Tilly
and the
Magic Potion

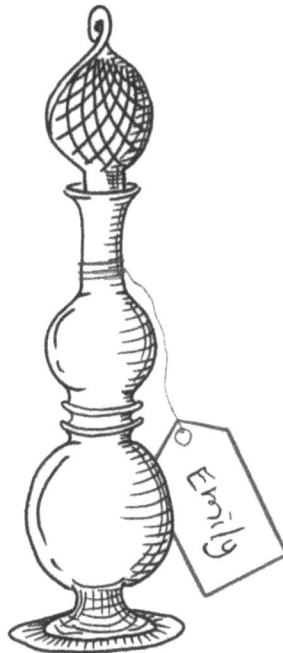

Books by the Author

Archetypes, Unmasking your true self (Balboa Press, 2017)
The Queen (Possumwood Publishing, 2017)
The Knight (Possumwood Publishing, 2017)
The Princess (Possumwood Publishing, 2019)
Self-Esteem Matters (Possumwood Publishing, 2015)
Decoding the Afterlife (Possumwood Publishing, 2015)
Fear Not (Possumwood Publishing, 2018)

Fiction

Charlie the Cheeky Spider (Possumwood Publishing, 2018)
Fantastic Adventures, What would YOU do? (Possumwood Publishing, 2020)
Tilly and the Magic Potion (Possumwood Publishing, 2020)

Tilly
and the
Magic Potion

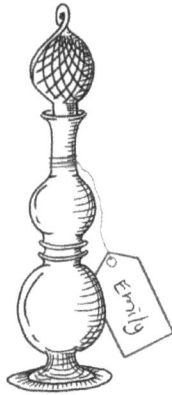

Emily

Brian Dale

Illustrated by M D Blackhall

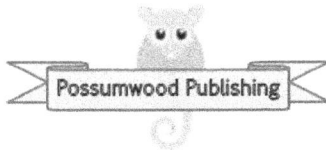

Possumwood Publishing

Possumwood Publishing

5 Possumwood Place, Mullumbimby, NSW 2482

Australia

possumwoodpublishing@gmail.com

First published in 2018

Copyright © Brian Dale, 2018

Dale, Brian

Magic

Witches

Death

Family

Illustrations by M D Blackhall

Cover photography by Jade L Dale

Typeset by Jan Dale

Printed by Clark & Mackay, Brisbane, Australia

Published by Possumwood Publishing

Dedication

This story is dedicated to the memory of Tahla Kathleen Dale who passed away on 15th March, 2013 at the age of thirty-three. Tahla was the loving daughter of Brian and Robyn, sister to Adam and Jade, and aunty to Luca, Lilly and Isla. Tahla was fiancé to Adrian and welcomed into the Cannata family, best friend to Marie, and companion to so many of her family, her extended family, her clients and friends.

Tahla had the amazing ability to blend and mix ingredients to make all kinds of magic potions. Her beauty therapy and natural skin care products reflected this aptitude. Good witches make magic potions and Tahla was both a good witch and a maker of magic potions.

This is a story told to Tahla's dad. It tells of another time when she was young and an inexperienced witch. It is her gift to the many children who believe in magic and who live in, or on the fringe, of their imagination. It is a gift to the many children who loved and adored Tahla and knew her as the kind, glamorous and generous young lady who touched their lives.

This is the first book in the 'Tilly' series. In the second book, *'Tilly in Mischief and Magic'*, the adventures continue, the adversaries grow more dangerous and Tilly and her sister Emily grow in power, knowledge and responsibility to battle the ever-increasing menace.

Tahla has now gone to Spirit.
However, her memory is
cherished forever by
her family and friends.

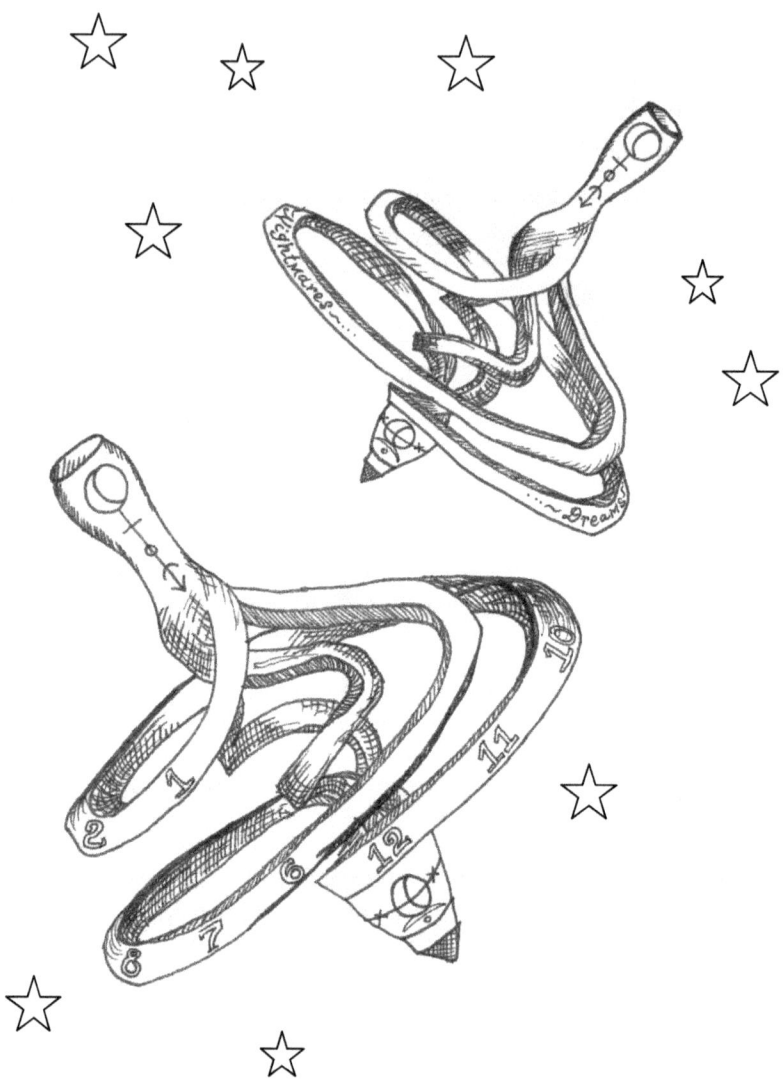

Chapter 1

Emily

Emily lay in her bed. Emily was ill. She had been ill for some months now. Emily did not understand why she was ill. The doctor said that her body had a disease. Most days she had to stay in bed. On other days, beautiful sunny days, she was strong enough to go walking.

Emily had always been on the frail side. People said her skinny legs looked like matchsticks. How they supported her body was a mystery although her body was also skinny.
Her long dark curly hair often fell across her face. She had a pixie face with blue eyes that sparkled when they met the sunlight.
She often peered from behind her hair to see what was happening. If there was somebody she liked she would push the hair off her face and greet them with a happy smile. If there were strangers she could stay in disguise until she was brave enough to meet them. There were some times when her face was always hidden.

Emily lived in a painted wooden cottage. The cottage was painted mauve with cream windows although there were places where the mauve and the cream had worn away to peeling and dirty boards.

The roof was made of tin. It was silver, once shiny, but now dulled by years of sunshine, frost and rain.

As with all people who lived in cottages, Emily loved the sound of rain falling on the tin roof. Listening to the rain drops splatter as she lay in bed was a comfort and safety Emily had always treasured.

Attached to the cottage letter box was an old, painted sign. It read 'The Happy House'. The words were adorned with butterflies but like the rest of the house they too had faded with age.

'The Happy House' cottage was surrounded with different neighbours. On one side, there stood a solid brick house. This belonged to Mr. Smead. Emily called him the man who lived next door because that is all she knew of him.

On the other side was a vacant block of land. Emily was never allowed in the vacant block of land.

Behind the cottage there were paddocks. When the grass was green and full of life, these paddocks were filled with cows. When the cold winter had chilled the grass to sleep or the hot summer sun had fried the green shoots to brown the cows were never seen nor heard.

A small garden wandered throughout the front of the cottage. It was the type of garden that came to life in the spring. Jonquils, daffodils and hyacinths led the flowers into full bloom and stimulating fragrance. These were followed by a dazzling array of colour presented by the different daisies, lavenders, foxgloves, geraniums, fuchsias and forget-me-nots. Most plants were held in by an old, knitted wire fence. Several flowers had escaped through the wire fence although they never made it past the footpath.

A wire gate led any visitors into the front garden. The gate was held in place by an iron arch. The iron arch was held in place by time, concrete and a tough jasmine climber. When the time was right the jasmine plant welcomed visitors with the wonderful sweet fragrance from its starry white flowers.

In recent times 'The Happy House' had become a little too small for Emily's family. When Emily became sick her brother and sister were forced to share a bedroom.

Josh was her brother. He was older than Emily and a lot braver. He was allowed to visit the vacant block next door. He would spend many hours climbing the trees and bashing a path through the undergrowth. When summer was at its hottest Josh would bring Emily blackberries which he had plucked from the wild blackberry bushes. He would come into her room; his arms dotted with blood and cuts from the blackberry thorns, and open his hands to reveal a dozen or so treasured blackberries.

"These will make you better," he would say to her. "Then I can have my bedroom back and you can put up with Tilly."

Tilly was Emily's little sister. Tilly did not understand many things.

"I can make you better," she would say to Emily. "I will mix you a magic potion. All I need is the right stuff to put in the potion."

"What sort of stuff do you need?" Emily asked her one day.

"Magic things!" she replied. "Willapa jumping berries, rainbow spotted toadstools and the flower of the Raggety Rascal tree! That will be the start of my magic potion." Tilly waved a stick in the air and her face smiled.

"Where will you find those things?" Emily asked. "I have never seen them around here."

"Oh! Some of them are close by and some of them are in another place." said Tilly.

"But how do you get to these places?" asked Emily.

"It is easy," said Tilly. "All you need is to hop, skip and jump. I will show you on the next moony night because you need to be outside under the big tree."

Tilly left waving her stick and practicing her hop, skip and jump. Emily lay in her bed and coughed.

Chapter 2

The Man Next Door

Mr. Smead lived next to 'The Happy House' cottage. Emily was afraid of Mr. Smead. She did not know why. In the two years Emily had lived in the cottage, she had never seen Mr. Smead.

In the first week of April, Emily was feeling well. She was allowed to walk in the garden. It was a good day. It was a happy day. Emily felt strong. The day was fine even though there was a little chill in the wind. Emily was walking down by the big, old fig tree. She noticed a bit of the fence was missing. There was a hole in the fence. It was only a small hole but Emily was sure if she peaked through the hole she could see into Mr. Smead's back yard. Mr. Smead had built a high wooden fence so that no one could see into his back yard. Emily began to walk towards the hole in the fence.

Suddenly a voice shouted, "Stay away, nosey parker."

Emily did not move. Then an eye peered through the hole.

"I am watching you," said the voice. "Stay away."

Emily's hair fell across her face.

She peered through her hair and noticed the eye move, like it was trying to spy on Emily and anyone else who could be there.

"And tell your little sister to stay out of my back yard."

Emily opened her mouth to speak. She would have said, "My little sister could not possibly get into your back yard."

But the words did not come. Emily stood there, her long dark curly hair covering her open mouth and surprised face.

Then the eye disappeared. The hole in the fence was covered. This was followed by a loud banging sound. It seemed to Emily that Mr. Smead had covered the hole with a piece of wood and was nailing the wood to the fence. The banging went on and on. Mr. Smead went to a lot of trouble to make sure the hole in the fence would never be open again.

When the banging stopped, Emily thought it would be safe to move.

Now she understood why she was afraid of Mr. Smead.

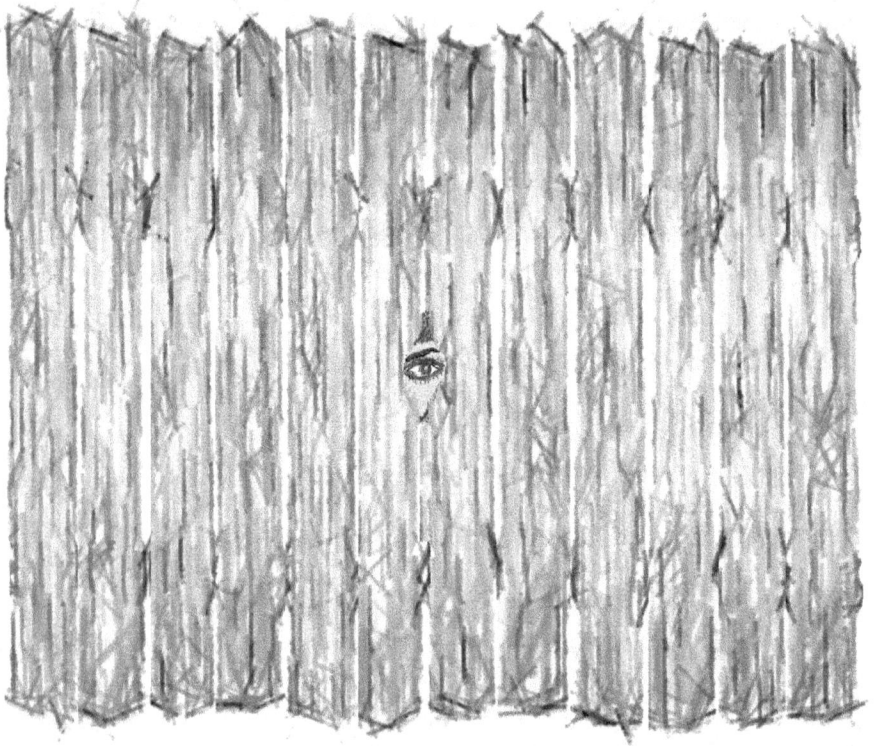

The Dream

That night Emily had a dream. Tilly had come into her room.

"It's time to go," she said.

"Where are we going to?" asked Emily.

"We are going to make magic," replied Tilly.

"Can't we make magic here?" asked Emily, rubbing the sleep from her eyes.

"You never listen to me, do you?" said Tilly.

Emily lay in her bed.

"Of course I listen to you," she thought.

Then she said, "I'm sorry Tilly. You have come to make magic and that is very good of you."

"I told you we need stuff," said Tilly as she folded her arms across her chest.

"Do I have to get dressed?" asked Emily.

"Your dressing gown and boots will do," said Tilly, "but we must hurry before they wake up."

Emily climbed out of bed and walked to the chair to find her dressing gown. She was going to ask, "Before who woke up," but decided not to. She put on her dressing gown and slipped her feet into her boots.

The two girls walked quietly out of Emily's bedroom, down the hall to the back door. Tilly led the way. She opened the back door and they went silently out into the cold night air.

"This way," said Tilly.

The night was still and the moon shone brightly.

For some reason or other Emily found herself creeping rather than walking. It was all very strange.

"Oh, well!" she sighed. "This is a dream and dreams are always strange."

Emily followed Tilly to where the big, old fig tree stood. Suddenly Tilly stopped.

"Whatever you do," said Tilly. "Never say umptidoodle."

"I promise," said Emily looking at Tilly with a face that looked like the man in the moon.

"And I hope you have been practicing your hop, skip and jump," Tilly said. "Are you ready?" she added.

"I suppose so," thought Emily.

Tilly grabbed hold of Emily's hand.

"I'll help you," she said. "We hop to the right, skip to the left and jump into the air."

Emily found herself staring at the big, old fig tree. Then her feet hopped to the right, they skipped to the left and she jumped high into the air. It was like flying. She felt as light as a feather as she soared over the fence and right into Mr. Smead's back yard.

"My goodness," she said. "That was umpti…" But she never finished as Tilly's hand pushed against her mouth.

"No talking," whispered Tilly. "Now, follow me."

They crept across the back of Mr. Smead's yard. They stayed in shadow, close to the back fence. Soon they came to a small tree that was twisted and wobbly-looking. Emily looked closely at the tree. By the light of the moon Emily thought she saw a face. The face was in the very middle of the tree trunk, and not a pretty face either.

"Up there," said Tilly. "I'm too little but you can reach if you stand on my back."

Emily looked up, glad to remove her gaze from the tree trunk. There on a twisted branch was a tiny purple flower.

Then she noticed that Tilly had knelt on all fours.

"Don't be silly," said Emily. "I'm too heavy to stand on you."

"Don't be silly, yourself," replied Tilly. "You have to."

Emily lifted her leg and placed one foot in the small of Tilly's back.

"I will hurt you," she said to Tilly.

Tilly turned her head upward and frowned at Emily. Emily had seen that look before and knew that nothing would change Tilly's mind.

"Oh, well!" she thought.

Emily pushed her foot down hard on Tilly's back and lifted herself off the ground. Tilly was like a rock. Emily found her balance, stood on tip-toes and reached up to pick the flower. Just as her hand neared the flower her whole body began to wobble. She felt like a jelly.

"Come on, Emily," said Tilly. "You can do it. Just go with the wobble. Go with the wobble."

Emily wobbled.

"Come on," she said to herself. "This is just a dream. Pretend you are on a tightrope. Now, get your balance."

Emily placed her left arm out to the side to balance her body then carefully and with great poise she reached up high and snatched the flower.

What followed was the most ear-piercing scream that Emily had ever heard. It seemed to come from the tree. The tree was shaking and the branches were rocking backwards and forwards and then from side to side.

Emily stood there in amazement until "whack" a branch took her legs out from under her. She crashed to the ground. She gasped at the cold night air and pushed herself up to a sitting position. She looked up only to see another branch swinging straight at her head. Then she felt a force grab her and roll her to safety. It was Josh. He pushed his face into Emily's.

"Good one, sis," he shouted.

Emily sat there panting. If only she could wake up. She wondered if she should pinch herself. She didn't have time to wonder for long. She saw from the corner of her eye a bright light. It was moving back and forth. Searching! Searching for intruders! Searching for her! Thoughts raced through her head but her body stayed still. Then, she felt a big hand take her right arm and a little hand take her left arm.

"Time to go," said her brother.

"You thieving little brats," yelled a voice.

Emily knew at once who the voice belonged to.

"You won't get away with this."

Emily found herself running. Then all at once she hopped to the right, skipped to the left and jumped high into the air. The moon shone on the three silhouettes flying high over the fence. Much to her surprise Emily landed lightly on her feet. She gathered herself and ran to the back door as if someone was chasing her. All she could think about was jumping back into the safety of her bed so that this very strange dream would end.

The next thing Emily remembered was waking to sunlight streaming through her bedroom window. She lay there safely snug in her bed. Slowly her bedroom door opened. Tilly entered.

"I knew you'd be awake," she said.

Emily looked at her little sister.

"I had the strangest dream," she said to Tilly.

"Really!" said Tilly.

Tilly walked over to Emily and very carefully prized open her right hand. A small purple flower lay there. It was in perfect condition, neither creased nor bruised.

Tilly took the flower and very gently placed it in a small cloth bag.

"What makes you think it was a dream?" she said.

With that, Tilly walked out of Emily's room and Emily stared at the emptiness in her hand.

Poppy

For the rest of the day Emily felt tired and exhausted. She lay in her bed thinking. She had plenty to think about. Every so often she would stare at the palm of her hand. Then she would drift into sleep. This time she had dreams. She dreamt about chasing rabbits and riding horses. She dreamt about birthday parties and going to the movies.

Then she had the nightmare. She was being chased. Voices were screaming at her. "Thief," they cried. The voices grew louder and louder. Then the lights flashed. Huge, bright spotlights roamed through the dark places of her mind.

She awoke to a voice.

"Emily," the voice was saying. "Emily, wake up."

Emily sat upright and there in front of her was Poppy. She flung her arms around him and hugged him tightly.

"My, my, you are in a state. What did I do to get this kind of welcome?" Poppy said.

Emily slowly let go of Poppy and lay back on her pillow. Poppy was her grandfather. He looked old but, at times, acted like her brother. His face was creased and lined but his smile hid all the faults.

Emily began to relax. She looked at Poppy.

"I had a nightmare," she said.

"We all have nightmares at one time or another," said Poppy.

"Yes!" said Emily. "But this one was different."

"Different! Eh!" said Poppy.

"It was all very strange," said Emily.

Now that she was starting to feel comfortable her brain and her mouth began to work together. And it was easy to talk to Poppy.

"Last night I had a dream," she said. "Tilly took me next door into Mr. Smead's back yard."

"Mr. Smead's back yard!" repeated Poppy.

"That's right," continued Emily. "We jumped the fence, no; we kind of flew over the fence. Then Tilly wanted me to pick this flower which I did. Then the whole back yard seemed to scream and there were lights flashing and Mr. Smead was yelling. And just before you woke me up I had the very same nightmare. It was so scary."

"I would think it was," said Poppy.

"But the really strange part was this morning. Tilly came into my room and took the flower. She took the flower right out of my hand. So, Poppy! How could it have been a dream?"

"It does sound very confusing," said Poppy.

"I am in such a muddle," said Emily. "I don't know if it's because I'm sick or maybe I'm going mad."

Poppy ruffled Emily's hair and placed his arm around her shoulders.

"You may be sick, young Emily but you are certainly not mad," said Poppy. "I'll tell you what I'll do. I have something you may like. I'll bring it back tomorrow and I'm sure it will help sort out all your dreams and nightmares."

Poppy ruffled Emily's hair once more and began to walk towards the door. His walk was slow and his right leg had trouble keeping up with his left leg. Emily noticed the small stoop that had become part of Poppy's walk.

"Poppy," said Emily.

"Yes," he said as he turned to face Emily once again.

"Do you believe in magic?" Emily asked.

Poppy took a step towards Emily but his eyes gazed into the distance.

"Well," said Poppy as his hand rubbed the stubble on his chin. "Are we talking about real magic or are we talking about magic tricks?"

Emily thought for a while.

"I guess I am talking about real magic," said Emily.

"Good," said Poppy. "There is nothing as strong as real magic. Stay well. I'll see you tomorrow."

And with those words Poppy opened the door, waved goodbye and left.

Emily listened to his footsteps as they went down the hall and faded through the back door.

"There is nothing as strong as real magic," she repeated as her head slowly reached for the comfort of her pillow.

Emily gave a huge sigh.

"Real magic," Emily said to herself. "I wonder what real magic is," and with those words Emily closed her eyes, not to sleep but to consider and to imagine.

Real Magic

Emily began to think. Sometimes she thought to herself. Sometimes she spoke to herself. Sometimes she did neither.

"I know there are magicians," she thought. "They do magic tricks like pulling rabbits out of hats. There must be a secret part in the hat which hides the rabbit. Some magicians cut people in half. These people must be very clever and very small since there has to be two people inside the box. They must also be very brave because there would not be much room and the blade must be very close to them."

"But these magicians do not do real magic," she said. "They do tricks."

Emily gave her mind and her mouth a brief rest.

"So, what is real magic?" she began again. "Harry Potter can do magic but he is a wizard. He is like a magician but he is not real. Harry Potter is a character in a book, a made-up person in a made-up story."

Emily rested once again.

"Real magic," she said once more and she half expected a magical person to appear and give her an answer. Alas! No one did.

"So real magic must be when a real living person does something that we think cannot be done."

This thought pleased Emily. It seemed to be right. It seemed to make sense.

Emily's thoughts continued. "We all know that no one can walk on water and that if a real person walked on water then that would be real magic. I have seen a television show where some people, real people, walked on fire. I think they walked on burning coals rather than fire. Still that must be real magic."

A moth flew past Emily's nose.

"People can't fly," she thought. "Insects can fly. Birds can fly but people cannot fly. If they are in an aeroplane then people can fly but it is really the aeroplane that is flying."

Emily sat upright and pushed her hair away from her face.

"Wait a minute," she yelled. "If last night was real and not a dream then we did some real magic."

She sat there and thought some more.

"That can't be true," she thought. "I can't do real magic. I know Tilly is a little strange but she is young and she cannot do real magic. I guess Poppy must be wrong. I must be going mad."

Emily lay back down. She closed her eyes. She was tired today. Sleep would make her feel better. Sleep would rest her body and take the thoughts out of her mind. Her mind was a muddle. If there was real magic it belonged to other people, not to Tilly and certainly not to her. She was just starting to feel happy with this thought when there was a noise outside her door.

"Good one, sis," said her brother's voice from behind the door.

Emily sat bolt upright once again.

"You said that to me last night, didn't you?" she yelled towards the door.

There was no reply.

"Big brothers can be so annoying," thought Emily.

Although now, sleep for Emily would not come for several hours.

Dreams and Nightmares

When she finally got to sleep, Emily slept well. She wasn't sure how she could sleep well with all the thoughts in her head but she did. Maybe her illness had made her tired. Maybe all that thinking had made her tired. Maybe her adventure the night before had made her tired. But she didn't know if that was real or just a dream. She also didn't know if it was a dream or a nightmare.

Poppy came late that morning. His smile made Emily glow. True to his word Emily could see a package tucked under his arm.

"Is that for me?" she said with a hopeful smile.

"Hello to you, young lady," came her grandfather's reply. "And yes, this is for you."

Poppy walked over to Emily's bed. She found her strength and threw her arms around his neck and hugged him.

"I like that greeting," Poppy said.

Emily sat back on her bed and waited. Poppy passed her the package and both sets of eyes looked down upon a brown paper bag.

"Open it up," said Poppy. "It won't bite you, yet."

Emily slid something from the brown paper bag.

The something was a wooden box. Emily could tell this was no ordinary box. She could feel the softness of texture. She noticed the light oak colouring. The box was beautifully carved. On the top there were words neatly written in gold. They said, 'DREAMS AND NIGHTMARES'.

"Should I open the box?" Emily asked.

"Why not," replied Poppy.

Emily slowly undid a small gold latch at the side of the box. She did not know why but her hand began to shake. Very gently she lifted the top of the box half expecting to see a jack-in-the-box bounce up at her. Instead she saw a very gentle glowing light. The light came from a circle. The circle reminded Emily of an old-fashioned clock face except there was only one hand and where the numbers would usually be there were words.

Emily read some of the words: RESCUE, ESCAPE, PARTY, REWARD, FAMILY, RISK, FRIENDSHIP, HAPPINESS, DEATH. Emily stopped reading. Death! How could Poppy give her a game like this? Emily closed the lid of the box.

"I don't think I could play this game," Emily said.

"It does look scary," said Poppy.

"It says horrible things," said Emily.

Poppy looked at Emily with a knowing face and said, "It is a game called 'Dreams and Nightmares'. You understand that your dreams are filled with beautiful things and wonderful adventures. You also understand that your nightmares are filled with scary things and strange adventures. It is up to you if you want to play or not."

Emily sat there paused in deep thought.

Poppy gave Emily some thinking time then he continued, "If you believe in real magic you know you are always safe."

Emily was safe. She was safe in her bed. She was safe in her house, 'The Happy House'. She was safe in her back yard. She never really went to too many other places because she was sick. She was safe being sick.

No! That didn't sound right. Emily's face scrunched up in thought. Being sick was not being safe. Being sick was dangerous.

"How can I be safe?" Emily asked Poppy.

"As I have told you, if you believe in real magic you will always be safe," he replied.

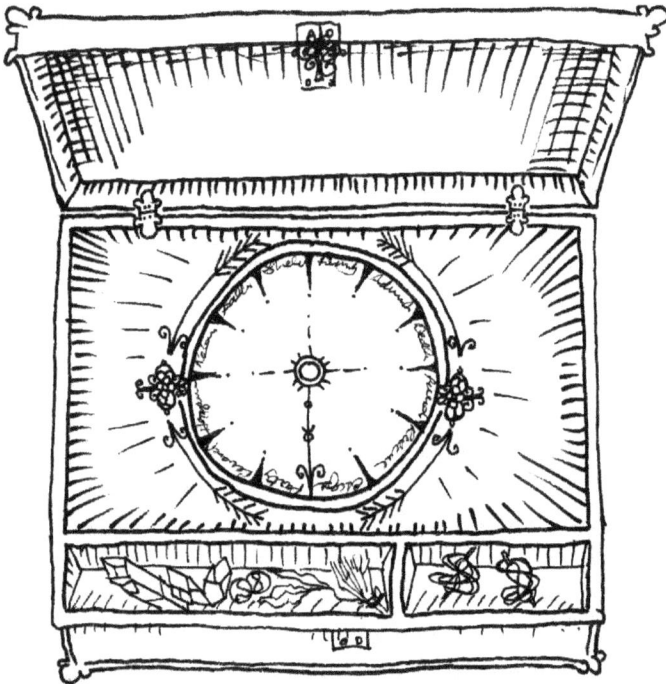

"Will you play the game with me?" Emily asked hopefully.

"I think you will find 'Dreams and Nightmares' is a game for one person," said Poppy. "You will understand that when you begin to play."

"I will have to think about it," said Emily. "It seems you would have to be very brave to play 'Dreams and Nightmares'. Josh is brave. Even Tilly is brave. I don't think I am that brave."

"You may just surprise yourself, young Emily," replied Poppy. "You never know what you can do until you put yourself to the test."

Emily sat there. There was so much to think about. Real magic! 'Dreams and Nightmares'! Being brave!

"I can see you have a lot to do," said Poppy. "I shall leave you for now and come back in a few days."

Poppy leant down to Emily and gave her a hug.

"There are many things we don't understand," he said. "It is all a matter of trust."

Poppy released Emily and left her deep in thought.

Life could be so confusing.

Chapter 7

Tilly

Emily stayed in her bed for the rest of the day. She placed the game, "Dreams and Nightmares" on her little side table. No matter what she did, she could not get the game out of her head. She tried drawing. She drew rabbits and horses. She drew fairies and toadstools. She drew many things but they all reminded her of her dreams. She tried reading. She read about knights and princesses. She read about dragons and six-headed monsters. She read about many things but they all reminded her of her nightmares. She tried to sleep but sleep did not come.

Late in the afternoon Tilly came into Emily's bedroom.

She was wrapped in her fake fur coat. Her long blonde hair was matted at the back. Tilly had never liked to brush her hair.

"I know where they are," she said to Emily.

"Where, what are?" Emily asked.

"The rainbow spotted toadstools, of course," was Tilly's stern reply.

"He thought he had hidden them but I am smarter than he thinks."

"Tilly!" said Emily.

Tilly was waving her stick in the air and mumbling words she had made up. Tilly was always making things up.

Emily was fond of her little sister but she did worry about her.

"Tilly!" Emily said again. "Have you been going into Mr. Smead's back yard?"

Tilly continued to wave her stick and mumble words.

"It is wrong to go into other people's yard without asking," Emily said.

"I have asked," said Tilly. "He wants me to come."

Emily took a deep breath.

"Did you go into Mr. Smead's yard the other night?" At last! Emily had asked the question that had been on her mind for two days.

"We all went in to Mr. Smead's back yard," Tilly replied. "We had to."

"We had to?" questioned Emily.

"You are a silly sausage," Tilly said. "I told you what we needed to make magic. You do want to get better, don't you?"

"Of course I want to get better," Emily said.

"Good!" said Tilly.

Tilly skipped around the room. Tilly hopped around the room. Tilly jumped around the room. Emily sat in her bed.

"Tilly," Emily said. "Do you believe in magic?"

As soon as Emily asked the question she felt very silly. She already knew the answer.

Tilly stopped. She looked sternly at Emily.

"Why, of course I do. You know that but what we really need to know," she said staring straight into Emily's eyes, "is; do you believe in magic?"

And with that Tilly waved her stick and skipped out of the room.

Chapter 8

Bravery

Emily stayed awake for many hours that night. Maybe it was Tilly that kept her awake. Little sisters are not meant to question their big sisters. Little sisters are meant to be the babies. Emily's conversation with Tilly made her feel like the baby.

Maybe it was the game sitting on the side table. Emily tried to take no notice of the wooden box but her eyes would be constantly drawn to it. Her thoughts would wonder; should she play this game of 'Dreams and Nightmares'? Was she brave enough? Josh would be brave enough. Even Tilly would be brave enough.

Emily thought of other things. Birthday parties! Did she believe in magic? She thought of her best friend, Josie. Josie was on holidays but would be back in a few days. Did Josie believe in magic? Did Emily believe in magic? Emily thought of Poppy. Poppy believed in magic but did Emily believe in magic. 'Real magic', that's what Poppy had said. Did Emily believe in real magic?

Emily finally slept with the question of real magic filling her mind. As families went about their nightly business there was no mention of magic, real or make-believe. As other children of Emily's age settled in for a good night's sleep their thoughts were on the latest song on You Tube or how much credit their phone had. Yet, as it had done many thousands of times before, the moon travelled across the night sky and, at dawn, the darkness would yield to the light of the sun.

Emily woke up in a sweat. It was almost dawn and a new day would begin. Emily felt better in the daytime. She felt braver in the daytime.

Emily turned over to stretch. There was the game 'Dreams and Nightmares'. She was staring at the wooden box.

"If you are so brave then play the game," said a voice inside her head.

"I'm not scared. I can be brave," said Emily.

Slowly she sat up in her bed. She reached over and took the wooden box in one hand.

"I will be brave," said Emily.

She switched on her side lamp just in case she needed to read the instructions. The extra light also made her feel braver.

Emily opened the wooden box. She looked carefully at the clock-face circle. Once again it glowed with a dull light but this time it seemed to hum. The hum was steady and even and inviting. Emily looked at the words. She read the words slowly. This time she read all of the words; even the ones that scared her.

"I am brave," she said.

There was something else in the box. There was a small spinning top. It was red with gold lettering. It had two words written on it; one word was **DREAM**; the other was **NIGHTMARE**. At the other end of the box was a larger spinning top. This top was purple and also had gold lettering. It had the numbers one through twelve written on it. There didn't seem to be any instructions on how to play the game. Then Emily saw a button. The button was flashing red; a long slow welcoming flash. When it flashed; the words '**PUSH ME**' appeared.

"I am brave and I can do this," Emily said to herself.

Her hand reached out and she pushed the button. The game came to life. The box played a short musical tune; the clock face lit up brightly and the tops stood tall and straight.

"You can still change your mind," said the voice inside Emily's head.

"No," she said to herself. "Poppy gave me this game to play. I trust Poppy. I will be safe. I will be brave."

Emily took the small top and held it between her thumb and forefinger. She spun it carefully and held her breath. The top spun merrily. Emily continued to hold her breath. The top began to slow. It hit the side of the box and came to a halt. One side of the top hit the bottom of the box and the word 'DREAM' began to flash. Emily let out a very big sigh.

Emily now felt excited and very brave. She took the big top with her thumb and forefinger and spun it with a smile. It seemed to spin for a very long time then all at once it landed on the bottom of the box and the number 2 lit up. Then all the lights in the box went out. The only sound was a humming but this time it sounded different. It was like the game was thinking. Then the hand of the clock spun wildly before coming to a sudden stop. The word 'ADVENTURE' lit up the clock face. Emily couldn't remember seeing the word 'adventure' but it must have been there. Then another light began to flash. It was green. Emily had not seen this light either. She pushed her finger forward to touch the light. The box stopped humming. The lights stopped flashing. Everything stayed still.

"Is that all that happens," thought Emily. "That can't be it."

Emily pushed the 'PUSH ME' button again. Nothing happened. Emily shook the box a little. Nothing moved and still nothing happened.

"That is strange," she said quietly to herself.

Emily placed the box on the side table and stared at the ceiling. Light and shadows began to dance. Emily felt very tired. She closed her eyes.

"Silly game," she thought. "All that time worrying for nothing."

Chapter 9

Statues

Emily woke to a sunny morning. Her mother brought her breakfast. Poached egg on toast with a side serve of cheese, mushrooms and spinach. She didn't really like spinach but she ate it to please her mother who reminded her how good it was for her.

After breakfast Emily looked across at the wooden box. It lay open. She couldn't remember if she had closed the lid or left it opened. It didn't matter. The game didn't work. She would have to tell Poppy when he next came to visit her.

By the afternoon Emily felt strong and she was allowed to walk in the garden. She wandered down to the back fence where the big, old fig tree grew. There was a ladder standing against the tree. No doubt Josh had left it there. Emily was not allowed to climb ladders because of her illness. Tilly was not allowed to climb ladders because she was young and small. Josh was not allowed to climb ladders because Emily and Tilly were not allowed to climb ladders. Josh thought this was silly so every so often he would sneak the ladder from the shed and climb to the lowest branch of the old fig tree. Emily was happy to see that Josh had forgotten to put the ladder away. This Sunday she felt extra strong. She climbed the ladder and sat on the lowest branch of the fig tree.

Emily was enjoying the view. She could see the spire of the church. She could see a few cows eating grass in the paddock beyond the back fence. She could see rooftops and chimneys and other trees but most of all she could see into Mr. Smead's back yard. Emily was not a rude child. She was not a nosey child. However, Emily was pleased she could see over Mr. Smead's high fence and into his back yard.

In the light of day Emily noticed that Mr. Smead's back yard was different. There were some things you expect to find in a back yard.

A curved path led to a shed tucked away in the back corner. Several metres in front of the shed grew the tree. Emily looked carefully at the tree. Its branches hung limp and the leaves flopped. It looked a most unhappy tree. Emily wondered if she was the cause of this unhappiness. What did Tilly call this tree? Emily couldn't remember. There were lots of things that Tilly spoke about that never made sense to Emily. Emily whispered "sorry" to the tree and moved her eyes elsewhere. The path separated the yard into two sections. On the far side was a vegetable garden. On the side nearest to Emily's yard was grass. There was nothing unusual about this until something moved.

Emily sat there. Her eyes were fixed on a patch of grass. It wasn't the grass that was interesting. It was the object that rose out of the ground, through the grass and sat there like a statue. This statue was black, wore a pointed hat and held a broomstick.

Emily couldn't believe her eyes. She rubbed them vigorously and looked again. A statue of a witch stood strong and bold in Mr. Smead's back yard.

"Why would Mr. Smead have a statue of a witch?" Emily said quietly to herself.

The statue was looking straight at Emily. Fortunately the witch's hat was extra large and fell half way down her face covering her eyes. Emily had a strange feeling this witch did not have a pleasant face or eyes that anyone would like to see.

Just as Emily was getting used to the thought that Mr. Smead had a statue of a witch, she noticed further movement.

Out of the ground rose a skeleton.

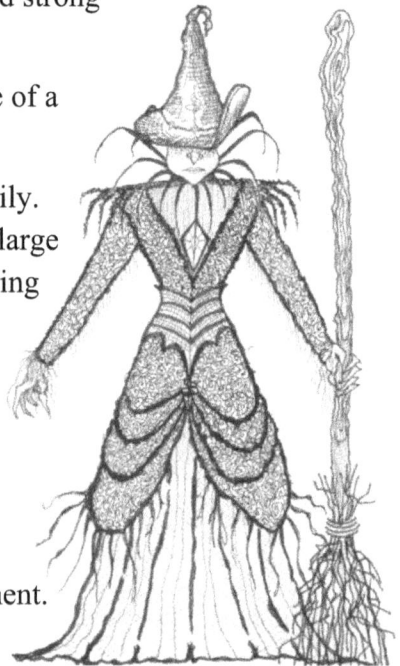

Emily was very interested in skeletons.

Poppy had given her a thick book about the human body and she was very keen on the part about bones and skeletons. Emily stared at the skeleton. It was very different from the pictures she had seen in her book.

This skeleton looked as if it could spring to life at any moment.

"How silly," Emily thought. "There is no such thing as a live skeleton. Well, there was but they were on the inside of people's bodies."

Emily had no time to consider this thought any further as her attention was drawn to another statue emerging from the ground. The witch and the skeleton were strange and scary, but this one was terrifying. This one was a giant praying mantis. It was twice the size of the witch and its face was looking straight at Emily. Emily moved her head and her hair covered her face.

Through the strands of her hair Emily could still see the praying mantis. Its eyes were enormous. They were blood red eyes with huge black eyeballs. Its mouth was crooked and cruel-looking which gave its face a scowl. Six legs attached themselves to a thin but muscular body. The two back legs looked powerful as if belonging to a body builder. The front legs were shorter than the other four legs but looked agile and threatening. A pair of pincers was attached to the end of the front legs. Emily didn't know enough about praying mantises to say whether they had pincers or not. This one certainly looked like it did.

As Emily sat there staring at the objects, out of the corner of her eye, she saw something else move. The something else was Mr. Smead.

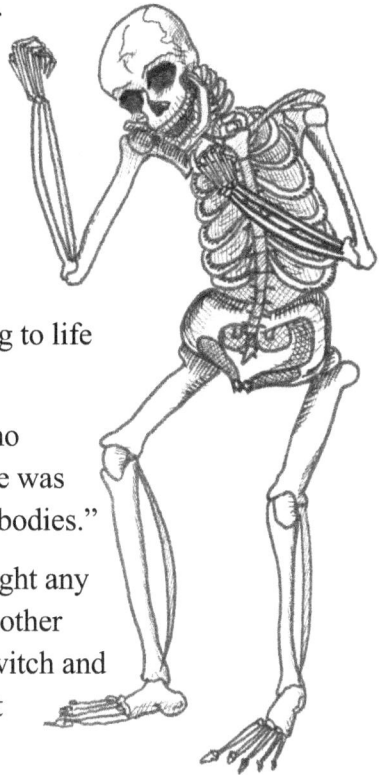

Emily had never seen Mr. Smead before, apart from one eye through the fence. She was not able to see much of him this time either.

Mr. Smead was draped in a black cloak. He did not walk like most adults do. He did not run as most children do. He was sneaking on his tip toes. He sneaked from his back door and stepped onto the path. As he sneaked down the path he looked all around as if somebody was spying on him. Emily had this funny feeling in her tummy. She was looking at Mr. Smead but she was not spying on him.

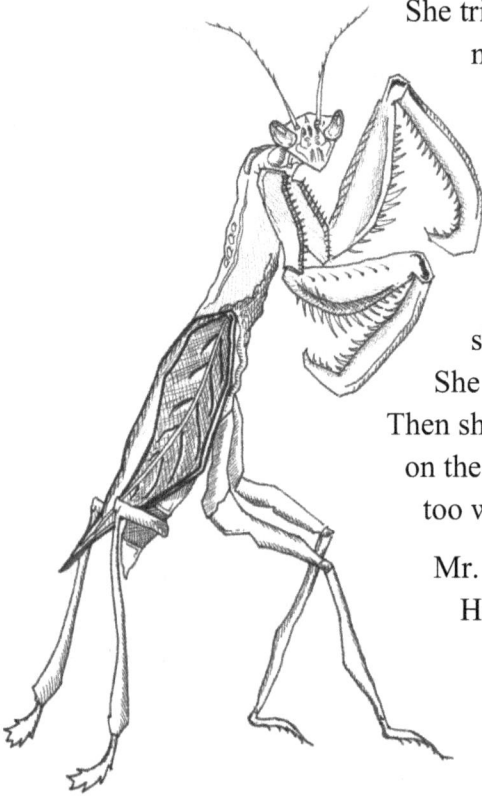

She tried to hide herself but that was not easy. Mr. Smead took the path towards the shed.

Suddenly he stopped.

He stayed very still. Emily felt her tummy wobble. Then, she thought she saw the skeleton move. She knew that was ridiculous. Then she thought one of the eyeballs on the praying mantis blinked. This too was ridiculous.

Mr. Smead began to tip-toe again. He came to the back shed. He looked all around, opened the door and went in. The door closed silently behind him.

Emily began to relax. She thought about climbing back down the ladder until she saw something move. She pushed her hair to one side and peered into Mr. Smead's back yard. Something had changed. The skeleton had gone; disappeared.

She looked carefully at the other two statues in Mr. Smead's back yard. One by one they sank back into the ground, first the witch then the praying mantis. Like sprinklers that had finished watering the garden they popped back into the earth. The difference was that these statues were big; two were the same size as Emily while the third was much bigger. Yet they disappeared smoothly into the ground. When the last one had gone the shed door opened. Mr. Smead came from the shed and searched his back yard. When he was happy that the statues had gone he began to creep back to the house.

Half way across the yard he stopped. He sniffed the air like a wild animal sensing danger.

Suddenly he turned and stared straight at Emily. He slowly raised his arm and pointed at her.

"I see you," he shouted.

Emily's heart raced. Her foot reached for the ladder. She felt the top rung with her left foot but her right foot felt nothing but thin air.

"Help me," screamed a voice.

It could have been Emily. It sounded like a voice from deep inside Mr. Smead's house.

Then Emily's head went blank. She heard nothing. She saw nothing. She knew nothing.

Jungle Fever

Emily was falling. She was falling fast, faster than she had ever fallen before.

Then she remembered to pull her rip cord. Her parachute sprung into life. Emily's heart stayed still while her body rose sharply to the beat of the air. She glided. She floated. She steered and then she landed.

Emily had landed in the middle of a patch of grass. She looked around her. She was surrounded by jungle. To her surprise her friend, Josie ran to her.

"Well done," Josie said. "Take off your chute. Zala will bring all the gear back to our camp."

Zala grinned at Emily with white teeth and a huge smile.

"We do not have long before sunset and we must gather the flower before then," said Josie.

Emily did not feel at ease yet she knew exactly what Josie was talking about. She slid out of her parachute gear, put on the backpack that Josie gave her and together they walked from the clearing to a track leading directly into the jungle.

The jungle smelt fresh and wet. Recent rain and only the glimmer of sunlight caused their path to be a little slippery. The track, however, was mostly clear. Every so often Josie would use a small machete to trim a low branch or a vine that blocked their path. Emily kept one

eye watching Josie's feet. Josie's walk was strong and steady. Emily kept her other eye looking right and left for any sign of danger. Emily knew the jungle well. This came as a surprise to her. If only she had the time to think about it.

They walked steadily for nearly an hour. Then they heard a sound very familiar to them. It was the roar of water. This was powerful water falling from a great height. They walked for a few more metres and the path opened out onto a small clearing. The clearing was on one side of a river. Slightly upstream, the river was battered by a waterfall. Water tumbled over solid rock and crashed into the river. The spray splashed randomly over river bank and jungle growth.

"There it is," said Josie.

She pointed to a small tree. The tree was twisted and wobbly-looking. Emily knew of this tree.

"Right up near that top branch is what we are after," said Josie.

Emily strained her eyes and caught a glimpse of something small and purple.

"How are we going to reach way up there?" asked Emily.

"My plan is for you to distract the tree while I climb quickly up on those branches."

"What a foolish plan that is," shouted a voice.

Emily and Josie looked around. They saw nothing.

"I think it is a very good plan," shouted Josie.

"You will be crushed before you get half way up," replied the voice.

"Show yourself so we can judge your advice," shouted Josie.

A boy emerged from the jungle. His chocolate-brown skin and curly hair suggested he was a local to this part of the jungle. He was wiry but muscular. Fashion played no part in this boy's wardrobe. He wore shorts that were worn and tatty and a t-shirt that had a slogan designed by a far-away city slicker to amuse the horde of city dwellers. He looked several years older than Emily and Josie but he was still a boy.

"Do you know what tree that is?" asked the boy.

"Of course," said Josie. "That is the Raggedy Rascal tree."

"But it is not your garden variety," said the boy. "This is your jungle variety. This tree is wild and dangerous. Much more dangerous than you suspect."

"We will take our chances," said Josie.

"I suppose you are after the flower," said the boy.

"Of course," said Josie.

"You will never get it by climbing that tree," said the boy.

"If you are so smart," said Emily. "How would you get the flower, then?"

The boy looked at Emily. His eyes studied her face, her shape and returned to her eyes. He gave her a cheeky half smile.

"Pretty girl with dark hair plays an amusing game," said the boy.

Emily blushed. She hoped that her face was flushed from her trek through the jungle and her embarrassment disguised. She opened her mouth to speak but nothing came.

"I will play your game and get you the flower," said the boy. "But you should give me something in return."

"Yes!" said Emily, finding her voice. "There is always a catch."

"I will not ask for anything that you are not willing to give," said the boy.

This time his smile was broad and full.

"Then we have an agreement," said Emily.

"Go to the front of the tree," said the boy. "But stay out of its reach."

Emily and Josie looked at each other. They had nothing to lose with this plan. If it worked, they would have what they came for with no risk taken. The friends moved carefully towards the tree. Suddenly the tree's branches began to sway. Soon they were swinging wildly determined to hit anything that came within reach. Josie danced around as if to mock the wildly swinging branches. Emily stood there as if in a daze.

Emily's daze was abruptly broken by a whoosh as something flew past her head. It was the boy. He clung tightly to a vine as he flew down from a tall tree. He sailed past Emily and over the top of the wildly swinging tree branches.

Just as he flew over the tree he bent down and plucked the small purple flower from the tallest branch.

The tree exploded into an uproar of screaming and wailing. Emily blocked her ears as Josie grabbed her arm and pulled her back away from the tormented tree.

The vine swung high over the river and then back towards the bank. The boy let go of the vine, rolled several times then bounced to his feet.

Emily felt as if she should clap him. The boy looked as if he deserved a clap.

"You've done that before," said Josie in a very matter of fact tone.

"That may be true," said the boy.

He held out his hand to show a small purple flower. Emily stared at the flower. She had seen it before but couldn't remember when. It seemed a lifetime ago.

Josie reached out to take the flower. The boy pulled back his hand.

"We made a deal," he said.

The boy stared straight into Emily's eyes. His stare made her feel self-conscious and she turned her head away to conceal a smile.

"We swap the flower for that necklace," the boy said calmly.

The boy pointed to Emily's neck. Her hand reached up and touched a silver chain. It was adorned with a small heart. Emily had no idea where the necklace had come from.

"You cannot have Emily's necklace," said Josie.

"Then you cannot have the flower," replied the boy.

Josie and the boy stood staring at each other. There was silence.

Emily knew the flower was important.

"I do not mind," said Emily as she undid the necklace, placed it in the palm of her hand and extended the agreed gift to the boy.

The boy took it with a grin.

He then placed the flower carefully into Emily's hand and with a strong but gentle touch folded her hand over the flower. Emily's heart pounded like it had never done before.

"Be careful how you use it," said the boy.

"We know what we are doing," said Josie.

The boy smiled. He began to walk away back to the jungle.

Emily was not ready for goodbyes.

"Thank you for your help," said Emily.

"At your service any time," said the boy.

"What if we need you again?" said Emily.

Josie turned her eyes and looked at Emily in disbelief.

"Then I shall be there," said the boy.

"Do you have a name?" asked Emily.

"Azamatea," was the reply and the boy disappeared.

Chapter 11

The Accident

Emily opened her eyes. She saw a sea of familiar faces. Her mother stood there, looking worried. Poppy sat in a chair, looking thoughtful. Josh was pacing and looking angry. Tilly was skipping around the room, looking as if she didn't have a care in the world.

"Where is Azamatea?" said Emily.

Her mother lent over her bed and hugged her gently. Then she kissed her forehead.

"Azamatea," said Poppy. "I haven't heard of such a place."

"It's not a place," said Emily. "Azamatea is a boy."

"You must have been dreaming," said her mother. "You had a nasty fall," she added.

"No!" said Emily. "I was parachuting and landed in the jungle, and Josie was there, and we met this boy who got me this strange flower. I gave him my necklace."

Emily stopped speaking. She looked at her family. She looked at the room she was in. It was not her bedroom.

"Where am I?" she asked.

"You are in hospital," said her mother. "You fell off the old fig tree because some naughty boy left the ladder there."

Emily's mother looked at Josh. Josh opened his mouth to say something but thought better of it.

Emily sat in silence. She remembered sitting on a branch of the big, old fig tree. She remembered looking into Mr. Smead's back yard. Then she remembered the statues. She began to shiver.

Her mother held her tight.

"That's enough for now," she said. "You've had a nasty fall but now you are safe in hospital. I have to ring your father and tell him the good news. Dad! Make sure these two behave themselves."

Emily's mother reached into her handbag and left the room.

"I'm grounded for two weeks because you fell off the ladder," said Josh.

"No," said Poppy. "You are grounded because you left the ladder out."

Josh walked away and sulked in the corner.

Tilly looked up at Emily. Emily looked at Tilly. Emily knew that Tilly wanted her to say something.

"Have you been in Mr. Smead's back yard again?" Emily asked.

Tilly stared at her.

"What have you two monkeys been up to?" asked Poppy.

"Nothing," said Emily.

She was not very good at telling lies and she hoped Poppy would not see through this one.

"I can see you have been playing 'Dreams and Nightmares'," Poppy stated.

This time Emily had to tell the truth.

"I think I had a dream," she said.

"Good!" was all, that Poppy replied.

Emily's mother came back into the room.

"Your father is so happy that you are awake and smiling," she said.

She bent over and kissed Emily on the cheek.

"That's from dad," she said. "Now we have to go but Dad will be here shortly. Push the button if you need the nurse."

Emily's mum kissed her on her forehead once more. Poppy squeezed her hand.

"You'll be fine, young Emily," he said.

They walked towards the door. Josh followed. There was no smile on his face. Tilly stood there.

"You saw the statues, didn't you," she said.

Emily gazed at Tilly. It was like Tilly had a power that forced her to answer.

"It was so strange. They went into the ground," she said with amazement.

"So that's where he hides them," said Tilly, more to herself than to Emily. "We have to stop him, you know," she added.

"Tilly!" called their mother.

"We have to stop him before he can make them come alive," Tilly said as she walked to the door. "You do not need to worry. I'll take care of them."

With those words Tilly left the room.

Emily sat there. She was sore. Her leg ached. She must have fallen on that leg. Her shoulder was also sore.

She was confused.

"What was a dream and what was real?" she thought.

She didn't want to think about Mr. Smead and the statues. They scared her. She did want to think about her jungle adventure. She seemed safer there, with Josie and with Azamatea.

"He was a strange boy," she thought.

She smiled when she thought of him flying through the air. Her smile grew wider when she thought of him holding her necklace. She shivered when she remembered the touch of his hand upon hers.

"I shall be there," he had said.

And with those words of comfort Emily lay down to rest.

Happy Talk

Emily wondered about her dreams. She came to the understanding that her time in the jungle must have been a dream. The game that Poppy had given her must work. It was not broken as she had thought. She remembered what Poppy had said.

"Good," was his reply when she told him that she'd had a dream?

She wanted the game but it was in her bedroom. She longed to be back in the jungle. She was not sick in the jungle. There was no falling off ladders, or seeing statues, or being scared by Mr. Smead. There was freedom and adventure in the jungle.

Her thoughts were interrupted by a nurse. The nurse smiled and gave Emily a cheery greeting. Then she went about her duties. She took Emily's temperature. She took Emily's blood pressure. She wrote on Emily's chart. She asked Emily about her leg and her shoulder. She asked Emily about her illness. She asked Emily if there was something that Emily wanted, maybe an ice cream.

"Can you ring our home?" Emily asked.

"I can do that," said the nurse.

"Can you ask my Pop to bring the game to me?" said Emily.

"Of course," said the nurse. "You need something to play with to keep you relaxed and stop you from becoming bored."

With that the nurse left the room.

Emily placed her head on the pillow and rested. She tried not to think about Mr. Smead and what was in his back yard. She tried not to think about how she managed to get into his back yard and about what she had stolen. She tried not to think about Tilly. Emily always worried about Tilly. So Emily thought about the jungle. Her thoughts were happy thoughts. Her thoughts were calm thoughts until she thought about the flower. The flower in her dream was the same flower she had stolen. Her heart began to beat fast.

Just then her father entered the room. He greeted Emily with a big smile, a big hug and words that took Emily away from her thoughts of flowers.

Emily and her father chatted for almost an hour. They talked about past birthdays and presents. They talked about holidays and things they had done together. They talked about things that made Emily smile. This was happy talk.

Their happy talk was interrupted by Poppy. He had brought Emily the game. Emily thanked him with a big smile and a big hug and the happy talk continued. The happy talk went on for almost another hour. The nurse came into the room to check Emily once again. Another helper brought Emily her evening meal.

Emily's Dad and Pop left her with smiles, hugs and words of comfort. The nurse finished what she had come to do and told Emily that if she wanted anything to push the buzzer. Emily ate her evening meal. Until then she didn't realize how hungry she was.

When she finished eating, Emily placed her tray on a table and pushed the table to one side.

Now Emily was alone. She was all alone with her thoughts once again.

Poppy had brought the game. Was she brave enough to play? She longed to be back in the jungle. This longing gave her courage.

She reached over and placed the wooden box on her lap. She opened the box and pushed the button. The game came to life. Emily reached for the small top and spun it with expectation. It landed on 'nightmare'. Emily's heart sank.

"Be brave," she told herself.

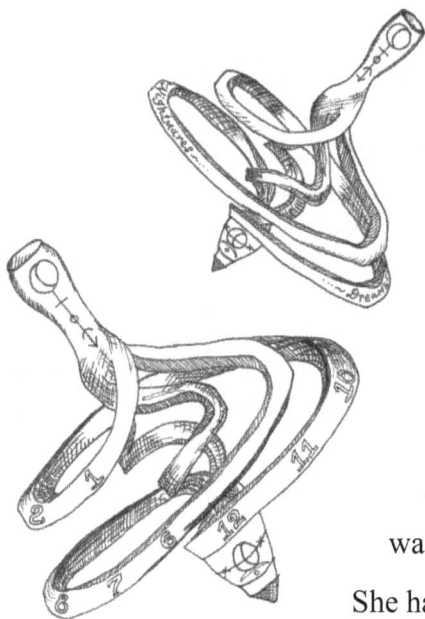

She took the big top and spun it hopefully. She watched it spin. She watched it land on the bottom of the box. She saw the hand spin wildly and the clock face light up the word 'PRISONER'. Again she had no memory of reading that word.

Emily knew the game would work in its own time. She closed the box and placed it on the side table. She felt tired and sore. She was also worried. Was it safe to sleep?

She had no choice as sleep came quickly.

Captured

That night there were clouds in the sky. They hid the moon. If the moon had been shining it would have shown a small girl sneaking out of her house. That small girl was Tilly.

Tilly shone her torch on the path leading to the big, old fig tree. There was no ladder leaning against the tree. The ladder had been locked away. Tilly did not need a ladder. Tilly knew magic. She hopped a little to the left. She skipped a little to the right. Then she jumped. She jumped right over the fence and landed in next door's back yard.

When she landed Tilly stayed perfectly still. She looked around. Not a thing moved. Three statues were standing on the grass, scattered throughout the yard.

Tilly thought she was safe so she began to relax. She didn't notice a pair of eyes looking at her.

Tilly began to creep along the back fence. This was something she had done several times before. This time the eyes watched her.

Tilly came to a shed. She walked past the shed and into a vegetable garden. She bent low to the ground. She dared not turn on her torch. She would have to feel her way through the garden. Slowly she crept. Her hands led the way.

Tilly did not notice that something else was creeping. This something looked like a huge praying mantis. Its feet moved silently over the ground. Its blood red eyes were focused steadily on the small girl crawling in the vegetable patch.

Tilly stopped. She thought she heard the movement of a foot. She slowly turned her body and strained to listen. Then she felt something brush against her knee. She carefully felt with her hands. She trembled with excitement. She forgot about the sound she thought she heard. She was too busy taking out a small pocket knife and slicing through soft flesh.

A gentle rustling sound filled the air. The sound floated to Tilly's ears. She turned her head upwards. Two huge eyes were staring at her. They were not human eyes.

Tilly stood to run but strong legs lifted her into the air. She waved her arms and kicked her legs but the creature held her tightly.

She grasped her pocket knife firmly and tried to plunge it into her attacker's leg. The knife made a metallic sound, bounced off her attacker and fell from her hand onto the ground.

The creature lifted Tilly higher into the air and then walked towards the shed. The shed door opened and Tilly was thrown inside. She rolled across the floor and bumped heavily against a chair. The chair crashed to the ground. Tilly lay there trying to catch her breath. The shed door slammed shut. Tilly heard the creature walk away. The only sound to be heard was Tilly struggling to breathe.

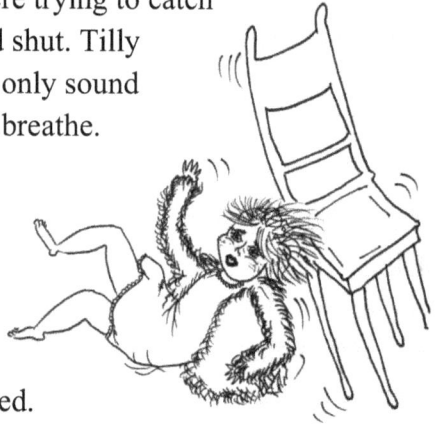

Emily awoke with a scream.

"Tilly," she screamed.

Tilly did not answer.

Emily sat up and looked around. She was in bed. This was not her bed. Then she remembered. She was in hospital.

The room was filled with light and a nurse rushed to Emily's side. Emily threw her arms around her.

"My sister has been captured," she said.

"There, there," came the reply. "You must have had a nightmare. Everything will be alright."

Bad News

Emily could not return to sleep. She could not even rest. She needed to know if her nightmare was real. Even though it was early morning the nurse gave in to Emily's request and agreed to call Emily's parents.

"Someone will be here shortly," said the nurse when she re-entered Emily's room.

There was nothing Emily could do but wait. She waited patiently. She waited impatiently.

Emily looked at the game 'Dreams and Nightmares'. She hated that game. Yet she loved her dream.

"It should have been called 'Just Dreams' or something else like that, then, when you played, you would only have wonderful adventures." she thought. "Why do we need nightmares and other scary things?"

If Emily had been allowed out of her bed she would have paced the floor. Instead, she pulled her legs to her chest. She pushed her legs out straight. She wriggled her toes. She pulled her legs to her chest again.

The door to her room opened. Poppy and Josh entered slowly. Emily took one look at Poppy's face and knew there was bad news.

"She's not in her room, is she," said Emily.

"What do you mean?" said Poppy.

Like Emily, Poppy was not good at telling lies. He had the sort of face that didn't suit lying. Poppy had an honest face. At least Emily could hide her face behind her hair. Poppy did not have that option.

"Tilly," said Emily. "I know she is missing."

"There is nothing to worry about," said Poppy.

Unfortunately for Poppy his face said there was plenty to worry about.

"Tilly has probably gone for an early morning walk," said Poppy. "You know what Tilly is like."

"Yes," said Emily. "I know what Tilly is like. I also know she is missing and I know exactly where she is."

Poppy's hand touched Emily's shoulder.

Josh rushed to Emily's bedside.

"Where, where is she?" he said excitedly.

"She is locked in Mr. Smead's shed," spluttered Emily.

Poppy gave Emily a very serious look. Josh gave Emily a look of pure excitement. He forgot all about how angry he was with her.

"I had a dream," Emily said. "No! I had a nightmare. This big mantis thing came and grabbed her and threw her into the shed. It was horrible."

"We have to rescue her," shouted Josh.

"Now you just hang on a minute, young fellow," said Poppy. "You just can't rush into other people's houses and accuse them of kidnapping. Besides," he added. "If I remember rightly, you are grounded."

Emily gave Poppy her most serious look.

"I am not telling a lie Poppy," she said.

"Of course you are not," said Poppy. "But there are some things that must be handled with careful consideration."

"But we have to rescue her," said Emily.

"That's right," added Josh.

"You leave it to me," said Poppy. "I'll come up with a plan."

Emily gazed at Poppy. She turned her serious face into one with half a smile.

Poppy glimpsed that half smile.

"We had better go, Josh," he said. "We have a young girl to find."

Poppy gave Emily a hug.

"Now, don't you worry, young lady," he said. "I'll take care of everything. I'll let you know the minute we find her. You have to rest. That's your job."

Poppy walked out of the room.

"Don't worry, sis," said Josh. "I'll rescue her."

Josh winked at Emily and rushed out of the room. Even though there were times when Josh could be a pain, there were other times when Emily thought he was the best brother in the world.

Emily sighed loudly then went back to wriggling her toes and waiting impatiently.

Waiting

Emily had never felt so empty. There was nothing she could do but wait. Emily hated waiting. It seemed that for all her life she was waiting. She waited for birthdays. She waited for Christmas. She waited to catch the bus. She waited to see her friends. Now she was waiting to get better. But worst of all she was waiting to hear about Tilly. She wouldn't wait any longer.

Emily reached for the game and sat it on her lap. She opened the lid and stared at the spinning tops.

"Do not let me down," she said.

She pushed the 'ON' button and the game sprang to life.

"Don't you dare let me down," she said once again.

She took hold of the small top and spun it with hope.

"Dream," she said to herself. "Give me a dream."

The top banged against the wall of the wooden box and came to a stop. The word 'NIGHTMARE' flashed silently.

"I hate you," Emily screamed.

She sat there in silence. Then she thought about Tilly.

Emily held her breath. She grabbed the big top and spun it with all her might. It spun with pace and anger. Then it stopped and the word 'RESCUE' flashed before Emily's eyes.

"Rescue, that is good," she said to herself.

But 'nightmare' caused her to shudder.

Emily knew the game would be played. She could not stay awake forever. She wanted to sleep and sleep now. She wanted this part of the game to be over. She wanted Tilly rescued no matter how scary the adventure might be.

Emily was not a bad girl but she needed help and help she would get.

She rang the buzzer for the nurse and asked if she could have something to help her sleep. The nurse knew Emily was not well. She knew that Emily hadn't slept much during the night. She also knew that Emily's family was busy with other worries. So the nurse gave Emily some medicine.

Emily waited impatiently.

"Rescue," she said to herself.

She said the word over and over and soon she fell fast asleep.

Chapter 16

Rescue

There was a polite knock on Mr. Smead's front door. An old man and a young boy waited on the front porch. There was no movement from inside the house.

The young boy grew impatient. He knocked on the door again.

Nothing! For a third time there was a knock on the door.

This time, the young boy saw movement from inside the house. He knocked a fourth time.

The door half opened.

"Yes! What do you want?" said a man with a growl in his voice.

"We were wondering if you had seen a small girl. Her name is Tilly," said Poppy.

"I've already told the police I've never seen the nosey pest," said the man behind the door.

"I don't believe you," said Josh.

"Believe what you want," growled the man as he shut the door firmly.

Josh went to knock again. Poppy grabbed his arm.

"But that was a lie," said Josh.

"I know it was," said Poppy.

Josh looked up at Poppy. Josh's young face was filled with anger and puzzlement. Poppy's older face was filled with understanding and determination.

"You know Tilly is a nosey pest. I know Tilly is a nosey pest. But how does a man who says he has never seen her know that she is a nosey pest," said Poppy.

"What are we going to do, Pop?" said Josh.

"There is only one thing left for us to do," said Poppy. "We will have to rescue her."

Josh smiled at Poppy. It was a smile of pure delight.

☆　☆　☆　☆　☆　☆　☆　☆　☆

Emily tossed and turned for almost an hour.

When her body and her mind finally relaxed Emily found that: *She was in the jungle. Her friend Josie led the way through a narrow jungle track. Emily watched the feet in front of her. She watched for the signs of danger. She seemed to know the jungle well.*

Emily loved being in the jungle. "This must be the most beautiful rainforest in the world," she thought to herself.

Her mind began to wander. She looked at the tall, solid trees that reached up to catch the sunlight. She wondered about the thick, strong vines that clung to those trees. She felt her feet tread through the leaf mulch. She thought about a boy she had met in the jungle.

"What was his name?" she wondered.

Emily's thoughts were interrupted by a sudden shout.

"Watch out," yelled Josie.

Emily saw the trap at the last second. She went to move her foot but it was too late. Her ankle was grabbed by a thick rope and she was lifted high in the air. There she hung upside down dangling helplessly.

Josie looked up at her.

"Don't panic," she shouted.

"I'll find a way to get you down. They must have tied the other end of the rope close by."

☆ ☆ ☆ ☆ ☆ ☆ ☆ ☆ ☆

Poppy moved the ladder up against the big, old fig tree. Josh went to scramble up the ladder. He was stopped by Poppy, grabbing him by the scruff of the neck.

"Hold on there," said Poppy. Remember you are grounded."

Josh looked at Poppy with sad but determined eyes.

"However," he added. "I'm not… and the job has to be done so let's go find Tilly."

Josh smiled and scrambled up the ladder.

Poppy climbed up after Josh who had made his way along a branch of the big, old fig tree.

"Time to check out the lay of the land," Poppy said.

Josh looked at him with a puzzled expression.

"You just don't go rushing into battle," said Poppy. "You look and plan."

Poppy and Josh looked over the fence into Mr. Smead's back yard. In the back corner stood a garden shed. The door was shut tight and the lonely window had bars. To the front of the shed grew a small tree. Josh knew that tree well. It stood quiet and restful but Josh had seen this tree angry and violent. To the side of the shed there was a vegetable garden. It was lush and full of plants. Most of this veggie patch was in sunlight but there was a small section close to the side fence that was covered in shade. The rest of the yard was grass apart from a narrow path that led from the shed to the back door of the house.

Poppy tapped Josh on the shoulder and pointed. He pointed to some faint but strange foot prints. The foot prints led to the veggie patch to a place where some of the plants had been damaged. There was another set of prints leading to the shed and then to a place near the centre of the grass.

"Are we ready?" asked Poppy.

"Always," said Josh.

Poppy slid past Josh along the branch of the fig tree. Slowly and carefully he climbed down the fence. He stood still for a moment and looked around the yard. All seemed quiet. Taking small steps Poppy made his way towards the shed.

Without a sound a giant praying mantis rose from beneath the ground. Large blood red eyes followed Poppy as he crept closer to the shed. The praying mantis rubbed its front legs together. The pincers were at the ready. The monster had another victim in its sights.

Poppy reached the shed. He revealed a small but strong crowbar. He slid one end of the crowbar between the door and the door jam. He prepared himself to pull with all his might. Then out of the corner of his eye he spotted the danger. The giant praying mantis looked at him with evil eyes. Attack was written all over its face.

Poppy pulled on the crowbar. The door groaned. The beast that was the praying mantis stood on its hind legs. Poppy took a big breath. He gathered all his strength and pulled once again on the crowbar.

The praying mantis made its move but instead of walking it came crashing to the ground. It hit the earth with a thud. It lay motionless on the grass, useless and defeated with its hind legs bound together with thick rope.

Josh danced about the beast very pleased that his rope and his knots had done their job.

The shed door groaned for a second time but then split away from the wood that once held it firmly. Poppy burst into the shed. In the darkness he saw nothing. Then he felt the arms of a small girl wrap around his waist. He picked Tilly up and they hugged joyfully. Poppy began to carry Tilly out of the shed to freedom.

"Wait," she said.

Tilly wriggled from Poppy's grasp and rushed back into the shed. She fumbled in the half-light until she found her treasure. She grabbed it with delight and rushed back to Poppy.

"Got it," she said. "We can go now."

They scurried across the back yard. Poppy helped Tilly climb the fence. He quickly followed her. They found Josh still dancing but this time on the branch of the big, old fig tree. Without looking at the yard next door they climbed down the ladder and stood in the safety of their own back yard. They all puffed and panted and exchanged hugs and high fives.

"You had better put that ladder away," Poppy said to Josh.

"Why, of course," said Josh in a voice that belonged to someone far more polite than Josh had ever been?

☆ ☆ ☆ ☆ ☆ ☆ ☆ ☆ ☆

"I need to be more careful," thought Emily as she dangled high in the air.

It was lucky she had her good boots on as the rope had slipped tightly below her ankle. It was hurting but not cutting into her soft skin.

Josie was moving back and forth scanning each and every tree.

"I think it's looped to that tree," she shouted up to Emily. "But I can't see any way I can climb up to set you free."

"And that is why you need me," a voice shouted.

Emily looked to her left although it could have been her right as being upside down had briefly confused her. She spotted a boy high up in a tree.

"Azamatea," Emily said. "That's what his name is."

Azamatea clung to a vine and swung out into the air. He did this with ease as if he had done the same thing a hundred times before. He landed safely in the fork of a huge tree.

"This is what you are looking for," he said with a grin.

Azamatea held out the end of a thick rope.

"Stay calm, troublesome one and I shall release you to the ground," he shouted towards Emily.

Azamatea pulled out a large knife. He pushed the blade back and forth over the rope. Emily felt a jerk as the rope was cut but she didn't fall to the ground. Azamatea held on with amazing strength and then lowered Emily smoothly to the ground. Emily rolled to a sitting position and began to ease the rope off her ankle.

"Thank you," was all she could shout in the direction of her rescuer.

Her joy and her embarrassment were cut short.

"There they are," growled a voice.

"Give me back my flower," called a second voice that was even angrier than the first.

"Run," shouted Azamatea.

Josie took off down the jungle track. Emily sprang to her feet and began to follow.

"So it's you is it, you little troublemaker," growled the second voice. "This is the last time you'll interfere."

Emily heard the sound. It was more of a whoosh than a bang. Then she heard a cry. It was a cry of pain. Without thinking she turned to see Azamatea. He was falling. He hit the ground with a thud. The noise hit her heart like the blow of an oversized jack-hammer.

"Run," Josie shouted.

Emily ran. She ran as if her life depended on it. Maybe it did.

Josie and Emily ran solidly for nearly thirty minutes. Josie stopped and pulled Emily into the undergrowth. They sat there panting.

"They won't come this far," Josie said between gasps. "We are close to camp and the rangers will be on patrol."

Emily sat there. Her body ached. Her mind was numb.

She sat there thinking of that boy.

"Azamatea! That was his name."

Tears of sadness began to fill Emily's eyes.

☆　☆　☆　☆　☆　☆　☆　☆　☆

Emily felt a friendly hand on her shoulder. The hand shook her gently.

"Emily," said a voice. "Wake up. You are dreaming."

Emily opened her eyes.

Through her tears she saw she was in a room. Familiar faces were looking at her. One face belonged to Poppy. Another face belonged to her brother Josh. But there was a third face.

"Tilly," she cried.

Tilly smiled and Poppy lifted her up on to Emily's bed.

The two sisters hugged as if there was no tomorrow.

Emily's tears of sadness changed to tears of joy.

Chapter 17

Magic Potion

Emily had to pinch herself. It was true. This was not a dream. This was her life and on this occasion she was pleased to be so very much alive. She was sitting in her hospital bed hugging her little sister. She sighed and sat back in her bed.

Poppy sat in a chair and pretended to read his newspaper. Josh began to explore the room.

"I was so worried about you," Emily said to Tilly. "I had a horrible dream that you were caught by this praying mantis and locked in Mr. Smead's shed."

"I was," said Tilly.

Tilly didn't even blink.

"I asked you not to go there," said Emily.

"I had to," replied Tilly. "He asked me. Besides I found this."

Tilly opened her hand. She held a small paper bag. She grabbed Emily's hand and tipped the contents into it. Pieces of toadstool fell into the palm of Emily's hand. The pieces sparkled with colour. All the colours of the rainbow glowed into Emily's eyes.

"They are beautiful," said Emily.

"They are magic," said Tilly. "Now all we need are the Willapa jumping beans and we can mix the magic potion."

Emily was lost for words. She had so many questions in her head she didn't know where to begin.

Tilly collected the toadstool pieces from Emily's hand and placed them back in the paper bag.

At last Emily began to sort out her many thoughts.

"I know you have told me but what is the magic potion for?" Emily said.

"For you, silly, to make you better," Tilly replied.

Emily had a vague memory of that conversation.

"But what are we going to do about the monster statues in Mr. Smead's back yard?" asked Emily.

"We are going to destroy them," said Josh from the far corner of the room.

Emily hadn't realized that Josh was listening.

"How can we do that?" Emily asked.

"I am working on a plan," said Josh.

"He cannot make them work without the magic, you know," continued Tilly. "And I have his toadstool. He will have to wait until another one grows."

Emily looked at her brother then at her sister. Did she really belong in this family? Suddenly Emily felt scared.

"You are not going back into Mr. Smead's yard again, are you." she said sternly to Tilly.

"I have to," said Tilly. "He has the jumping beans."

Emily looked over at Poppy.

"Poppy, can you talk some sense into Tilly. Please don't let her go into Mr. Smead's yard." she pleaded.

Poppy lowered his newspaper. He gave Emily his most serious look.

"The one thing I have learnt dear Emily is that as you go through life, you have to do what has to be done," Poppy replied.

Emily sat there in silence. She couldn't believe what Poppy had just said to her.

"But Tilly is stealing," Emily protested.

"I am not stealing," said Tilly. "I have already told you he wants me to come."

Tilly was always difficult, sometimes she was impossible. Emily agreed to herself that this was one of those times when Tilly was impossible.

Mum and Dad entered the room and the conversation about stealing, jumping beans and 'what had to be done' finished. Instead, the next hour was spent in happy chit-chat, nothing serious. There was talk of movies and television shows. There was talk of friends and family. There was talk of the weather and past holidays. Mr. Smead and magic potions were put to one side. They would be back inside Emily's head soon enough.

Chapter 18

Treasure

Emily's family said their goodbyes at about four o'clock. She would have an early dinner as they do in hospitals and then get some rest. It had been a happy day but it had also been a tiring day.

Emily's thoughts turned to Tilly.

"Tilly would be safe," she said to herself. "Poppy will look after her."

No matter how many times she said Tilly would be safe Emily still had this feeling of nervousness and doubt.

"There is nothing I can do to help her," Emily said to herself. "I'm sick and stuck in hospital. Besides she won't listen to me anyway."

Emily's thoughts turned to her dreams and her nightmares. Since she had begun playing the game her dreams and nightmares seemed more real. She remembered her conversation with Poppy about 'real magic'. Were her dreams magic? Could her dreams come true? And if her dreams could come true no doubt her nightmares could come true also.

Emily's thoughts went to the jungle. Azamatea! Thank goodness she remembered his name. Azamatea was lying injured and captured. Once again Emily felt helpless. How can you rescue somebody when they are part of your nightmare? And how could you possibly go back to the same nightmare; even if you wanted to.

Emily lay in her bed and watched the darkness take over the world.

"It is good to sleep when the world is covered in darkness," she thought to herself.

Would she dare play the game tonight?

Of course she would.

Emily reached for the game and placed it on her lap. She felt calm. This time she was going to accept whatever the game gave her. Deep down she knew she had no choice.

The small top spun with vigor. It landed with a soft clunk and the word 'dream' shone brightly.

"Fantastic," thought Emily.

She spun the big top with hope and desire.

It landed with a heavier clunk and the word 'treasure' flashed before her eyes.

Emily's heart beat with joy.

"A dream about treasure," she thought.

"Maybe I'm a pirate and I lead my hearty crew to discover a hidden treasure chest. I wonder what a pirate would spend their money on. A new pirate ship, perhaps!"

Emily considered a place where you could buy a new pirate ship. She imagined it to be like a car yard only this yard would be in the water.

"I would walk up to the salesman and ask for the latest model in pirate ships. Maybe take it for a test sail. I'd have cash and would haggle for a good deal."

These thoughts made Emily laugh.

"I am silly tonight," she said quietly.

She would fall asleep chuckling to herself.

Emily dreamed.

She was back in the jungle. She and her friend Josie were hiding.

"I don't believe it," said Josie.

"What don't you believe?" asked Emily.

Josie pointed to Emily's right boot. Emily looked. Nothing special about her boots! But there was something special beside her right boot. It was a toadstool. Emily had seen this toadstool before but then it was in pieces. Here it was whole. Here it was magnificent. It shone the colours of the rainbow, layer upon layer upon layer. It was like a hologram, picture perfect.

Josie pulled out a knife and sliced the toadstool at the base of the stem.

"This is treasure," said Josie. "We have had a great day," she added.

"I guess we have," said Emily.

Josie could hear the lack of enthusiasm in Emily's voice.

"You are worried about Azamatea, aren't you?" Josie said.

"I would just like to know if he's alright," said Emily.

"There is nothing we can do tonight," said Josie. "We have to return to camp and get a good night's sleep. Maybe in the morning the rangers will have something to tell us."

Emily agreed. There was nothing that could be done that night.

Josie and Emily crawled from their hiding place and set out for camp along the narrow track. Emily, although tired, stayed cautious and alert. She was not going to fall into any more traps.

When they reached their camp, bed and sleep found Emily to be a willing customer. Tiredness blocked out the memory of Azamatea falling to the ground. Emily whispered a short prayer and fell asleep.

Rogues and Villains

The sun and the morning sounds woke Emily. She was refreshed. She stepped out of her tent to see a familiar face. Josie greeted her. Josie was always an early riser. Emily loved sleeping in.

Emily understood why she liked Josie as a friend. Josie was strong and athletic. She was forward and straight to the point. Her hair was a sandy colour and always cut short for convenience. Josie was so many things that Emily wasn't.

Breakfast is ready," Josie said.

Emily and Josie ate breakfast. After they had eaten there was a meeting. Josie's father, the head ranger, gathered his band together. They were chasing poachers.

Josie told of yesterday's adventures and discoveries. There was plenty of praise and congratulations for the discovery of the flower and the toadstool. Finding two treasures in one day was amazing. No one could remember such good luck and good hunting. The flower and the toadstool were vital in the research for fighting diseases. They would be taken back to a city laboratory where scientists could examine their curative properties.

After the compliments the girls were brought back to earth with a warning. Josie's father reminded them of the dangers and how they strayed too far from the base camp. His stern look told Emily to take his warning seriously. Yesterday they were lucky. Azamatea was not so lucky. Emily waited for the conversation to turn to the poachers.

Josie's father was taking his men to the south.

"After yesterday's meeting with the girls they will be heading out of the jungle as quickly as possible," he said. They have a good head start on us but their cargo will slow them down."

Emily was not so sure about this plan. These guys were ruthless. They were angry. Emily wondered if they would give up so easily. She made her thoughts known but it seemed she could not change anyone's mind.

Josie's dad looked at the girls.

"You can do some scouting today but stay near the camp," he said. "I have ordered Louis to stay with you."

The meeting broke up and everyone prepared themselves for the day's activities. Josie's dad and his band of four rangers went south in the hunt for the poachers. Three rangers stayed on guard duty at camp. Emily, Josie and Louis stood around the burnt out camp fire and considered their options.

Emily had a strong feeling. It sat in her gut and refused to move.

Josie looked at her friend. She could see the determined look on Emily's face.

"You really want to go to where we were yesterday, don't you?" Josie said.

"I think these guys are really annoyed and will hang around until they get what they want," said Emily.

After yesterday Josie was happy to let Emily have her way.

They gathered their gear and headed back down the track. Emily led the way with Josie in the middle and Louis bringing up the rear. Emily's senses were sharp. She noted every tree. She heard every sound. Every fibre of her being was on high alert.

They trekked steadily for about an hour. Louis suggested a rest. Emily did not want to rest but she knew she had to stay fresh and a small rest would do her the world of good.

They sat and ate and drank. They let their bodies relax and their minds run free. Emily thought of Azamatea. Was he still alive? Was he free or had he been captured? Would she ever see him again?

After fifteen minutes Louis called the girls back into formation. Once more they set out on the narrow jungle track. Emily put all of her attention back onto the mission. There were no more thoughts of Azamatea. She listened to the feeling in her gut. Her gut churned. She led them to a place where the track was joined by another smaller track coming in from the right. Emily stopped.

"We need to hide," she said.

The others looked at her. They listened. There was no sound of danger.

"Are you sure?" asked Louis.

"We need to hide," was all Emily could say.

Emily moved off the track and into the undergrowth. Josie and Louis looked at each other. It seemed that Emily had taken charge of this venture. They too scrambled into the undergrowth. All three sat there quietly. Emily sat there like a statue although her stomach spun like a whirlpool.

Time moves ever so slowly when you are sitting in silence, just waiting. Emily had no idea of what she was waiting for.

Then she heard a noise, faint at first but coming in her direction. Emily checked her hiding place. It seemed in order. The noise became voices. There were two voices, speaking freely. Soon after there followed the sound of humans walking through the jungle.

Two figures came into view. Emily strained to catch a glimpse. The leader was short and stocky. He had dark features hidden behind a week's growth of facial hair. Machete in one hand, rope slung over one shoulder he looked the type you see on a police mug shot. As he got closer, Emily could see a rifle slung over his shoulder. The second man was taller and leaner. He carried a cage. Emily couldn't see what was trapped in the cage but it was desperately trying to escape. They disappeared as quickly as they appeared.

Emily waited until they could hear the voices no more. She fought her way back onto the track.

The others joined her within seconds.

"We have to follow them," she said.

"Just give me a moment," said Louis.

Louis fiddled with some instrument. Emily didn't notice. She was too anxious to begin the chase.

"All done," said Louis.

Before he had finished speaking Emily was walking. There was purpose in her stride. Her mind was on full focus and her hearing on high alert. They walked for about twenty minutes until unfamiliar sounds greeted them.

They stopped and peered into the distance. There appeared to be a small clearing. They crept closer. The clearing was home to a camp site. Louis indicated to the girls to edge closer, see what they could and retreat back a hundred metres to talk about what they had seen.

Emily, Josie and Louis spread out and each made their own way forward.

Emily caught a glimpse of the two men they had seen on the track. They seemed relaxed, chatting quietly. The shorter one seemed to be smoking while the other had something in his hand, possibly a drink.

Emily scoured the perimeter looking for others. Surely they must have duty guards. Emily could see no other person, no other movement.

Wait! There was movement. Over to the left of the camp site there was movement.

Curiosity got the better of Emily. She moved stealthily. She crept ever so slowly and carefully to the left. She kept one eye on the two men and the other for any sign of danger. She understood the risk of her being found out but she needed to see what was making all the movement.

Finally she was rewarded. There were cages. Many cages! Cages of all sizes and they were filled with wildlife. In the bigger cages Emily could make out a spider monkey and a kinkajou. There appeared to be a number of birds including a scarlet macaw. To the side of the cages there were containers. No doubt they contained precious amphibians and reptiles.

The actions of the poachers filled Emily with rage.

Then she caught a glimpse of something else that had been captured. This animal had only two legs. This animal was also caged like a wild beast. This animal was a boy. Emily had found Azamatea.

Emily's rage leapt to new heights. Her body shook. She wanted to scream. She wanted to rush out and release all these trapped creatures. They were so beautiful. She wanted to grab these men by the scruff of the neck and throw them into a cage. They were so cruel. These men ...

The men were no longer sitting at their camp site. Anger had distracted Emily. She turned to retreat but was grabbed by a strong hand.

"Look who we have here," said a gruff voice. "You have my flower, Missy."

"Suck eggs," she replied and was rewarded with a slap over the head.

Emily was pushed into the clearing where the news became worse. Louis was being held captive by a stranger with a gun.

"How stupid," thought Emily? "Of course they had a guard and we were so careless. Maybe Josie escaped."

But there was no such luck. The short man emerged with Josie. She was also a prisoner.

The poachers had gathered their prisoners. Louis, Josie and Emily had their hands and feet bound together with thick rope. Each of them was then strapped to a tree.

Louis apologized to the girls. He was meant to keep them safe. Emily was more upset with herself than with Louis. She was so angry. She was angry with herself. She was furious with the poachers. She resented the people who couldn't care less about the animals. She was incensed at the world for being this way. Unfortunately, there was nothing she could do about any of these things.

After a while, the men began to pack. Emily wondered how they planned to leave the jungle. There was no road into the camp site and there was no motor vehicle to be seen. In fact there was nothing with wheels. Emily realized the poachers had planned their escape by air. A helicopter would have to be their means of transport.

The longer she sat there, the longer Emily slid further into anger and further into sorrow. She hated the poachers. They would sell these wonderful animals and probably make a handsome profit. No doubt, they would be back again. She wondered about the people who were willing to pay a lot of money to have these animals. They would have to be kept in secret. She would never understand their selfishness.

Emily was deep in thought when she heard a scuffle. She couldn't see what was happening. Were the poachers fighting amongst themselves? She caught a glimpse of the short man running towards the jungle. A gunshot filled the air and sent the surrounding wildlife into frenzy. The short man stopped and raised his hands.

Emily's heart pounded fiercely. What was going on? She scanned the clearing for other signs that gave her hope and comfort. They arrived in the form of Josie's father. Her heart filled with joy as he strode through the clearing to the place where the three captives were held.

"How did you know? How did you find us?" she blurted.

"It's a long story," was the reply. "But I placed my trust in you; Louis kept me informed as to your whereabouts."

Josie's father untied the binding ropes and set the girls free. He then turned his attention to Louis. Freedom, it was a magical feeling.

Emily walked into the centre of the clearing to where her captors had become the captives. She wanted to get a good look at the poachers. She wanted to look them in the eye and show them her disgust. The last one in line was the tall man who had caught her.

She looked straight into his face.

"Suck eggs," she said forcefully.

Chapter 20

We have to go Under

Tilly was a witch. She was a good witch, not the wicked kind you read about in story books. Tilly was making a potion for her sister Emily. Tilly had just returned home from visiting Emily in hospital.

Tilly needed three ingredients for her potion to work their magic. She had the flower from the Raggety Rascal tree. She also had pieces of the rainbow spotted toadstool. The last ingredient she didn't have. The last of the ingredients were Willapa jumping beans. Tilly didn't have any Willapa jumping beans but her neighbour Mr. Smead did.

When Tilly got home she went down to the back of her yard. A big, old fig tree stood in the corner. Tilly noticed something different about the big, old fig tree. There was a branch that reached out to the top of the high fence that stood between Tilly's back yard and Mr. Smead's back yard. That branch had been cut off. It lay in three pieces next to the tree trunk.

"That is strange," thought Tilly.

Tilly also noticed that the fence had been made a lot higher. Extra poles had been attached and at least twelve rows of barbed wire were strung between each pole.

Tilly thought about her 'hop, skip and jump'. Although she was a good witch, Tilly was also a young witch and the power of her magic was still growing.

"I'm not sure if I can jump that high," she said to herself. "Still there must be other ways to get into Mr. Smead's back yard."

Tilly went and found her brother Josh. She told Josh about the branch that had been cut down and the barbed wire.

"That man is rotten to the core," said Josh. "But he won't beat us."

Late that afternoon Tilly and Josh started work on their plan. It would have been easy for Josh to get the ladder and a pair of bolt cutters, place the ladder against the fence, cut the strands of barbed wire and climb down into Mr. Smead's back yard. The ladder and the bolt cutters were locked in the shed but Josh knew where the key was. However, Josh was in trouble for leaving the ladder out which added to Emily having a nasty accident. Josh didn't want to get into trouble again. Josh was a complicated boy. Instead of the ladder Josh got a spade.

"If you can't go over the fence then we shall go under the fence," said Josh.

While Josh dug Tilly started singing.

"We can't go over it. We can't go over it. We can't go through it. We can't go through it. We'll have to go under it. We'll have to go under it."

Tilly knew these words were not right but she didn't mind.

By dinner time Josh had dug a small tunnel under the fence. It only needed to be small because only a small person needed to fit through.

Josh and Tilly ate their dinner. They played for an hour or so before they were sent to bed. They sat in their beds and waited. Eleven o'clock found them sneaking out of the back door and making their way to the tunnel.

"Are you sure you know where they are?" asked Josh.

"I think so," said Tilly. "That man is smart but I am much smarter. What about the praying mantis?" she added.

If he hasn't got the toadstool then he can't fix it," said Josh. "I reckon it'll still be lying where it fell."

Tilly looked at Josh. It was nice to have a useful big brother. Then she crawled through the hole and under the fence. The first thing she noticed was that the giant praying mantis was just as Josh said it would be. It was lying on its side. Tilly went and poked it with her finger just to make sure it was useless. The beast didn't move.

Tilly made her way towards the veggie garden.

Suddenly the back yard lit up. Four big floodlights flashed down on Tilly.

"I was expecting you," said a voice.

Tilly shielded her eyes from the brightness and could just make out a man sitting in a chair.

"You really are a nosey pest," said the man.

"I am not," said Tilly. "I am a witch and a very good one."

"Well little witchy-pants, at the moment, you are trespassing," the man said with a smug look on his face.

"I am not," said Tilly. "I have come to get the jumping beans and Mr. Smead said that I could come and collect them when they were ready. They should be ready by now."

"They are," said the man. "But you see I need them more than you do."

"How could you?" said Tilly. "I need them to save my sister."

"Too bad," said the man. "I need them to make my inventions come to life. You have only met one of my inventions. I call him Stickly. Wait till you met my skeleton and my witch. By the way, my witch is not a good witch. She is a nasty witch."

"I need to save my sister," repeated Tilly.

"But I shall be the greatest and most feared magician on the planet," said the man. "So I guess it's your sister or me and as I have the jumping beans, I win."

"But Mr. Smead promised them to me," said Tilly.

"You shouldn't make promises you can't keep. That was always the problem with my brother," said the man.

"And you shouldn't lock your brother in his own home and keep him prisoner either," said a different voice.

Tilly looked at the speaker. It was Mr. Smead. He was standing by his back door and right next to him was Poppy.

"Tilly," said Mr. Smead. "This is my brother, Bertram. I'm afraid he hasn't been very nice lately."

Bertram stood up. He looked at his brother. He looked at Poppy.

"Well brother," said Bertram. "It has been a nice visit. Far too short but pleasant enough! We must do it again some time."

And with these words Bertram charged at Poppy. Poppy tried to stop him but Bertram was younger and stronger. He knocked Poppy to the ground and raced through the house to freedom.

"No," shouted Tilly. "We have to catch him. He has the jumping beans."

Mr. Smead ran after his brother but the night was dark and Bertram disappeared into the shadows.

Tilly ran to Poppy to see if he was alright. Poppy stood up gingerly. He would have a couple of bruises and maybe a cut but he would mend quickly enough.

Tilly hugged Poppy to make him feel better and Poppy hugged Tilly to make her feel better.

Poppy explained to Tilly about Mr. Smead and his brother, Bertram Smead. Mr. Smead and his brother Bertram are inventors. They worked together for several years. Just as they were about to make an amazing breakthrough with robots they had an argument. Bertram disappeared for two weeks. When he returned he did a terrible thing to Mr. Smead. Bertram locked Mr. Smead in the cellar and kept him there. Bertram wanted to use the robots for his own purposes. It was only when Poppy and Josh visited the house to ask about Tilly that Poppy realized something was very wrong.

"I knew you would be here tonight," Poppy said with a smile.

Their talk was interrupted by a most amusing sight. Josh was crawling under the fence. Unfortunately being a lot bigger than Tilly he became stuck.

"If you are not too busy," said Josh. "I could use a hand."

"I think a spade would be more useful," said Poppy.

Chapter 21

Making Arrangements

Emily woke up. She was exhausted. She looked around at her room in the hospital.

"Oh!" she thought.

She wondered if her dreams were becoming more real than her real life.

Her real life was illness. Her real life was hospital. Her real life was tiredness.

In her dreams she was fit and healthy. She had adventures. She had energy. She had vitality.

Even when breakfast arrived Emily struggled to eat.

"What, not hungry this morning," said the nurse. "You have to eat you know. You need to keep those energy levels up."

"I know," said Emily.

There was little enthusiasm in her voice.

Emily lay on her bed and thought. She didn't seem to be in the mood to think of happy things. Her adventures in the jungle made her happy but they were not real. Catching the poachers and rescuing the animals was not real. Azamatea was not real.

She was real.

Emily's thoughts turned dark.

"I have been ill for months," she thought. "I don't seem to be getting better. I wonder if I will ever be well again."

Emily sat there in silence. Her eyes caught a glimpse of her game, 'Dreams and Nightmares'.

Her memory wandered to the first time she opened the game box. She suddenly felt nervous. She remembered why she had shut that box. It was upon reading the word, 'death'.

Was she going to die?

"Young girls don't die," she said to herself.

But she knew young girls do die. Children die every day. It's just that people don't think about such things. Emily didn't want to think about such things either.

Fortunately her dark thoughts were interrupted as Poppy and Tilly entered her room. Emily gave Poppy the biggest hug her strength would allow.

"What did I do to deserve that?" he asked.

Emily didn't answer straight away. The dark thoughts came back to haunt her.

"Because you are wonderful and I love you," Emily said.

Tears filled her eyes.

Poppy placed his arms around Emily. She cried more tears.

The two of them sat there in silence. Emily let her tears flow till she could cry no more.

"Poppy," she said.

"Yes," replied Poppy.

"Am I going to die?" asked Emily.

Poppy sighed.

"We are all going to die," said Poppy. "None of us know when. That is the way it is, always has been and always will be. Now why would you ask such a question?"

"I have been sick for months. I seem to be getting weaker and weaker each day. I know I am having different medicines but nothing seems to be working," said Emily.

"Everybody is doing the best they can," said Poppy. "Nothing is for certain but we are all confident you will get better."

"I could have made you better," said Tilly.

Tilly had been so quiet that Emily had forgotten she was in the room.

"If only he hadn't stolen the jumping beans," growled Tilly.

"Who stole the jumping beans? Was it Mr. Smead?" asked Emily.

Poppy lifted Tilly onto Emily's bed and they told her all about last night's adventures.

"So the grumpy man was Mr. Smead's brother," exclaimed Emily. "That explains a lot of things."

Emily's dark mood lifted as she listened to Poppy and Tilly. She especially liked the part where Josh got stuck under the fence.

When all the talking was done Tilly gave Emily a very serious look.

"But he stole the jumping beans," Tilly said. "I have the flower. I have the toadstool. All I needed were the jumping beans."

"It will be alright," said Emily. "I'm sure you will still be able to make your magic potion."

"Not without the jumping beans," said Tilly.

"Right," said Poppy. "It's time we left. Emily needs her rest."

Emily felt tired and didn't argue.

Tilly and Poppy gave her a hug.

"Now you keep your spirits up, young lady," said Poppy. "Your Mum and Dad will be in soon and we shall see you tomorrow."

Tilly and Poppy left the room and Emily lay down for a rest. She was always a lot happier after seeing Tilly and Poppy.

Emily drifted off to sleep.

Emily's Mum and Dad came to visit her that evening. They smiled and chatted although Emily sensed that something was not quite right.

Emily had been asleep when they arrived. She thought she stayed asleep although she remembered that her Mum and Dad had talked to the doctor. Emily didn't hear or understand much of the conversation. There was talk about another drug. However, she did remember the doctor talking about making arrangements, just in case.

It was a strange thing to say, 'making arrangements'.

Chapter 22

Death

Emily awoke. She was hot and sweaty. Her breathing was strained. She didn't know what time it was although she thought it must be close to midnight.

She pushed her buzzer to call for the nurse. The nurse gave her something cool to drink. She took Emily's temperature, checked her breathing and gave her something to relax her and put her to sleep.

The dark thoughts filled Emily's mind once again. She had never thought about dying yet once again it was on her mind.

"Where do you go after you are dead?" she thought.

It wasn't a very nice thought and Emily decided to think about other things. She thought about Poppy and Tilly. She thought about their adventures. She missed being part of their adventures. How could she be part of their adventures when she was stuck in hospital? Even if she was out of hospital she had little or no strength to join in.

When she had adventures they were in her dreams. She reluctantly agreed they were also in her nightmares.

Emily felt exhausted. Her illness was draining the life force out of her. She thought about those words, 'life force'. She must have heard them in a movie. It was the sort of thing you hear in movies.

Emily felt drowsy. The medicine was beginning to do its job.

"I need an adventure," Emily said quietly to herself.

She strained and reached out to take the game. She opened the box.

Did she really want to play? Was she brave enough?

There was no time for thinking. She would be asleep shortly.

Emily pushed the button. She took the small top in her hand and spun it. The word 'DREAM' soon flashed before her eyes.

"Thank goodness," she whispered to herself.

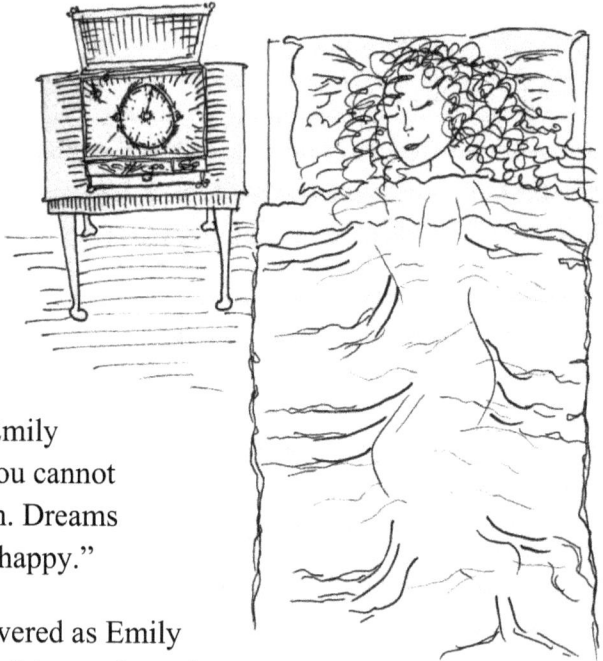

She took the large top and spun it. It barely spun several rotations.

The word 'DEATH' flashed painfully.

"But it is a dream," Emily said to the world. "You cannot have death in a dream. Dreams are nice. Dreams are happy."

The world never answered as Emily closed her eyes and fell into a deep sleep.

The Gift

Emily found herself in a tent. It was hot and humid. Sweat was dripping off her.

There was also a bed in the tent. It was a type of camp bed, not very comfortable. In the bed lay a boy. He was sweating even more than Emily. He had a fever. His name was Azamatea.

Emily looked at Azamatea's face. Even through the sweat and pain his face fascinated Emily. How was it that she, a girl not yet into her teens, could feel for this stranger? They had barely spoken yet she felt as if she knew him better than she knew herself. Her heart beat rapidly with a warmth and longing she had never before experienced.

Emily placed a cold towel on Azamatea's forehead. She took his wrist and felt for his pulse. It was weak and variable.

Emily placed Azamatea's arm gently by his side and began to pace. Her thoughts turned to anger. She was angry at the poachers. These men who capture and sell beautiful and wild animals deserve punishment. The rangers had caught three of them. The fourth would remain free. He was the helicopter pilot who realized at the last minute that something had gone wrong. Emily hoped his helicopter had crashed. The thought of death filled Emily's mind.

Emily felt exhausted. Once again she sat by Azamatea. She looked deep into his eyes and her anger turned to rage. Here was a young boy whose only mistake was to protect those beautiful and wild creatures that filled his world. He lay there with a gunshot wound and his life in the balance.

Josie quietly entered the tent.

"How's he going?" she asked.

"Not very well," was all that Emily could say.

Tears welled in Emily's eyes.

How could she feel this way? This boy had seemingly stolen her heart in the twinkling of an eye. He was only a boy. She had met him only yesterday. Yet he had her necklace.

"When will the chopper get here?" she asked in frustration.

Josie looked at her.

"Maybe within the hour," she replied.

Emily began to pace once more. Maybe her pacing could bring the helicopter here sooner. Maybe her pacing could rush the doctors and medicines here quicker. Maybe her pacing could give Azamatea more strength. Maybe her pacing could create a miracle.

Azamatea groaned.

Was it a groan of pain? Emily was not sure.

Azamatea opened his eyes. He smiled at Emily and touched her necklace.

Maybe Emily's pacing had created a miracle.

"Mm my bag," said Azamatea.

His voice was weak and strained.

Emily ran to the corner of the tent and grabbed Azamatea's bag.

Azamatea placed his hand inside the bag. He fumbled for a few seconds then smiled at Emily.

"Do you believe in magic?" he asked.

Emily dropped the bag.

"I guess I do," said Emily.

"No! You do not guess. You believe," said Azamatea.

Emily thought of another conversation. In another world, distant yet familiar!

"I do believe," said Emily. "I believe in real magic."

Azamatea took a deep breath and sat up. He opened his hand.

"These are for you," he said.

Azamatea handed Emily two beans.

"Willapa jumping beans," Azamatea said. "Tell her a lock of hair and thirty minutes."

"Thank you," was all Emily could say.

"Remember," said Azamatea. "I shall always be there."

Azamatea fell back onto his bed, took one more breath and then he breathed no more.

The tears rolled down Emily's cheeks and splashed onto the ground. The ache in her heart tore her thoughts into tiny pieces. She could say not a word as there was nothing to say. Silence filled the tent.

Emily's hand folded over and she clung to those beans as if her very life depended on it.

Willapa Jumping Beans

Emily woke up. She was hot and sweaty with fever. She looked into a sea of faces. Mum, Dad, Poppy, Aunty Jillian, Uncle Tom, her best friend Josie and Josie's mum and dad.

They all stood there staring at Emily.

"Good morning, sweetheart," said her Mum. "You have visitors."

Emily's visitors greeted her warmly. Josie came forward and gave Emily a huge, friendly hug.

"I thought you were on holidays," Emily said.

"We were," said Josie. "But we got bored so we decided to come home early."

Emily looked past her visitors. She scanned the room.

She was in hospital. Her brother Josh was in the corner pretending to fight monsters. Her sister Tilly was sitting on a chair. She looked like she was sulking.

Emily brought her attention back to Josie.

"I had the strangest dream," Emily said. "You were in it."

Josie took Emily's hand and tears began to form in Josie's eyes.

"What are these?" said Josie.

Emily opened her hand and saw two seeds.

"They are Willapa jumping beans," said Emily. "They are part of my dream."

Tilly sprang to her feet.

"Willapa jumping beans," she yelled.

"Shh, Tilly!" said her Dad. "You are in a hospital."

"You have Willapa jumping beans," shouted Tilly even louder.

"Show me," yelled Tilly at the top of her voice

Tilly pushed her way through the crowd of visitors and ran over to Emily's bed. She jumped up and down trying to see what was in Emily's hand.

"Yes," she yelled. "They are. They are Willapa jumping beans."

Tilly looked at Emily.

"Where did you get them?" she asked.

Tilly didn't wait for a reply.

"Never mind," she said. "It doesn't matter."

Tilly reached up and Emily handed her the jumping beans.

"You need a lock of hair and thirty minutes," said Emily.

"Where did that come from," she thought.

"A lock of hair, of course," said Tilly. "And thirty minutes!"

Tilly ran around the room.

"I need scissors," she said.

"Dad," said Emily's Mum. "Would you do the honours and deal with her?"

Poppy found some scissors in the top drawer of the bedside chest and handed them to Tilly.

"Come on, young lady," he said. "I'll take you for an ice-cream."

Tilly grabbed the scissors.

"Bend down," she said to Emily.

Emily gathered her strength and bent over the side of the bed. Tilly cut off a lock of Emily's hair. She passed the scissors back to Poppy.

"Forget the ice-cream," Tilly said. "We have to go home."

Tilly grabbed Poppy's hand and pulled him towards the door.

"Don't you go away," she shouted at Emily. "We'll be back."

Chapter 25

Friendship

"As if I am going anywhere," Emily said softly as she watched Tilly drag Poppy out the door. Emily managed a weak smile.

Then she looked at the people surrounding her bed. Their faces were strained. Their faces were nervous. Maybe she was going somewhere.

"Maybe I am going to … No!" Emily wouldn't allow herself that thought.

Emily looked at her friend Josie. She wanted happy thoughts. Emily thought of the good times she and Josie had shared. She thought of the tea parties in the big, old fig tree. She thought of rides on bicycles and picnics in the park. She thought of sharing swap cards and stickers. She thought of Josie protecting her from silly boys and their mischief. She thought of friendship and what it meant. She thought about the times when she was grumpy and angry and how Josie was always there with her.

Emily reached out and took Josie's hand.

"I haven't told you about my dream," she said.

Emily's voice was soft and fragile.

"We were in the jungle and we met this boy. His name was Azamatea."

"You met a boy," interrupted Josie.

"It was just a dream," said Emily. "I swapped him my necklace for a flower."

"Now that sounds like you, Em," said Josie. "You were always a loser for making bad deals."

Emily coughed a little then drew more breath.

"He had the most beautiful smile," she said.

Emily pictured Azamatea's face, his chocolate-brown skin, his mop of curly hair, his mischievous, brown eyes and his smile that flashed white teeth and lit up Emily's heart.

"He gave me the jumping beans just before …" Emily's voice trailed away.

At that moment the nurse came into the room.

"Sorry to interrupt," she said. "The doctor has a new medicine for our star patient."

Emily's family and friends stepped back from her bed. The nurse gave her two small pills which Emily swallowed.

"That will do the trick," said the nurse. "I'll just give you the once over while I'm here."

The nurse took Emily's temperature, checked her pulse and blood pressure and wrote on her chart.

"The doctor will be here in about an hour," she said. "You may need to get some rest, young girl."

The nurse smiled at Emily. She smiled at Emily's parents then left the room. Josie's parents made an excuse to leave the room and have coffee.

Josie returned to Emily's side and took her hand.

Emily wanted to talk but tiredness and her thoughts stopped her. She thought about Willapa jumping beans. She thought about her dream.

It was all so confusing. The medicine had made her instantly tired.

Emily drifted into sleep.

She felt the warmth of a hand holding hers. Sometimes the hand was the size of her hand; sometimes the hand was bigger, softer or rougher. But a hand was always there.

Magic Medicine

When Emily opened her eyes she looked into her Dad's face. He looked worried.

"Hi Dad," she said.

"Hi sweetheart," Dad said. "Did you have a good sleep?"

"Pretty good," said Emily. "How long have I been asleep?"

"Nearly two hours," said Dad.

"Where's everyone?" Emily asked.

"They've just gone down to the cafe for coffee and something to eat," said Dad.

"Dad," said Emily. "Do you believe in magic?"

Dad was not given the opportunity to answer.

Tilly burst through the door and into the room. Poppy followed looking totally worn out.

"Here drink this," said Tilly.

Tilly thrust a small bottle at Emily. It contained a coloured liquid.

"Wait a minute," said Dad. "What are you giving Emily? The doctor has just changed her medication and we don't want to interfere."

"It's a magic potion, Dad," said Tilly. "I told you it will make Emily better."

Tilly stared at Dad.

Tilly's Dad knew that stare. It was pure stubbornness and determination. It was a stare he had when he was Tilly's age.

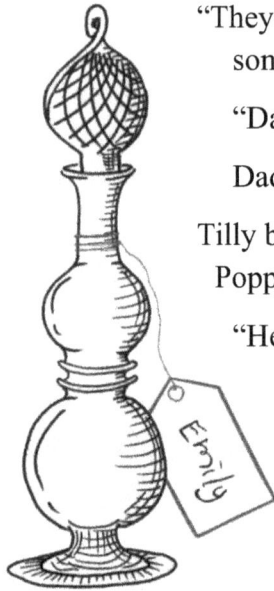

"Beats me, Jack," said Poppy. "She is a witch, you know."

Poppy's words brought a smile to Dad's face.

"Drink it," said Tilly and she took Emily's hand and placed the small bottle in it.

Emily looked at her Dad then she looked at Poppy. Poppy nodded "yes".

Emily took the top off the bottle and drank the potion.

She thought of Mr. Smead's back yard. She thought of the screeching and flailing Raggety Rascal tree. She thought of pieces of rainbow coloured toadstool. She thought of jumping beans. She thought of Azamatea. She thought of her friends and her family.

Emily smiled.

Tilly stood there, waved her stick and danced around the room.

Emily's visitors returned to her hospital room. They all looked refreshed and not quite so serious.

Josie's parents said their goodbyes and left quietly. Josie was allowed to stay. Josh had places to go, so Dad agreed to take him.

Emily's Mum sat on a chair and tried to read a magazine. Tilly wandered the room practicing her spells. Poppy pulled up a chair and sat by Emily's side. Josie stood next to Emily and held her hand.

"If you like you can tell me more about your dream," Josie said.

"It was magic," said Emily. "It was real magic," she added and she gave Poppy a knowing smile.

Chapter 27 **The Very Best Witch**

The doctor was impressed with Emily's recovery.

"The marvels of modern medicine," he said. "She can go home today but we still need to keep an eye on her."

Emily was looking forward to going home. She had been in hospital for two weeks. It had been the longest two weeks of Emily's life.

Emily's Mum came to collect her. They gathered all of Emily's things and said farewell to the nurses and hospital staff. Emily left with a wooden box tucked neatly under her arm. This treasure, she was not going to leave behind.

There was a happy crowd of well-wishers to welcome Emily home. They filled the lounge room and spilled over into the kitchen. There was chatter and smiles and good things to eat. They were all so busy with what was happening inside the house, they never noticed what was happening outside. If they had they would have noticed a man peering through the lounge room window. His face was twisted in anger. His eyes squinted and his hands turned into fists.

"Nosey pest," he repeated over and over until he grew tired of watching so many happy people.

He skulked his way to a gate and turned to face the small mauve cottage.

"Revenge shall be mine," he muttered through clenched teeth.

Then he saw the sign. It read, 'The Happy House'. The man banged the sign with his fist and walked off down the street. The sign swung happily back and forth. The rusty chain sang joyfully.

Back inside 'The Happy House' Emily sat in the comfortable chair in the corner of the lounge room. Usually Dad sat there.

Emily felt a happiness she had never felt before.

Tilly walked over to Emily. With her was a man Emily had never seen before.

"This is Mr. Smead," Tilly said.

"Pleased to meet you," he said to Emily while shaking her hand.

"Mr. Smead is a wizard," said Tilly.

"I don't know about being a wizard," he said. "But I am an inventor and my latest invention is a gate. This gate joins our back yards. From now on you will not have to use ladders or tunnels to come and visit me."

"He really is a wizard, you know," repeated Tilly. "He grew all those things I needed for my magic potion. And we might need them again."

Mr. Smead looked at Tilly. Then he looked at Emily.

"You have one very smart sister," he said to Emily. "And she really is a witch."

"I am a witch," said Tilly. "I am the very best witch. I made Emily better."

Emily nodded in agreement.

"But best of all," said Tilly. "Emily believes in magic."

Emily looked at her sister. She looked around the room filled with friends and family.

"I do believe in magic, real magic," Emily said.

Then Emily smiled. It was the happiest smile Emily had ever given.

It was a magical smile.

About the Author

Brian Dale is a retired primary school teacher and librarian. He is still very active teaching drama to primary and secondary students, telling stories, writing fiction and non-fiction books and facilitating archetype workshops for adults and teenagers. Through his knowledge of archetypal energies he has an amazing understanding of children, their interests and personalities.

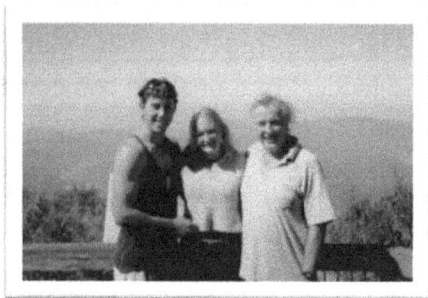

**Adrian, Tahla and Brian
Mount Warning, NSW 2012**

'Tilly and the Magic Potion' was written in memory of Brian's amazing daughter Tahla Kathleen Dale who passed away in March 2013.

Tahla was a beauty therapist of the highest integrity.

She had all the skills and attributes of a witch, in that she was able to conjure up the most incredible natural beauty products and assist her customers with inner knowledge and harmony.

Tahla was loved and adored by the children who filled her short but wonderful life.

Brian loves writing for children, especially books about fantasy. He enjoys teaching his drama students and observing their growth and development in their maturity and creativity. It is similar with the characters in the 'Tilly' series. As the stories progress each character grows in power, depth and maturity.

"That is the most rewarding aspect of writing fiction. Each character tells their story and as their story unfolds they reveal a little more of their personality. As an author you are the witness and scribe to that process."

www.ingramcontent.com/pod-product-compliance
Lightning Source LLC
Chambersburg PA
CBHW070534030426
42337CB00016B/2192